STUDENT GUIDE

Introduction to
MANAGEMENT
ACCOUNTING

Dudley W. Curry

Ph.D., C.P.A., Southern Methodist University

STUDENT GUIDE

7th Edition

Introduction to MANAGEMENT ACCOUNTING

Charles T. Horngren

Gary L. Sundem

Prentice-Hall, Inc., Englewood Cliffs, New Jersey 07632

Editorial/production supervision by Linda Marie Scardelis
Cover design: Jayne Conte
Cover photograph: John Scowen, FTG
Manufacturing buyer: Ray Keating

Printed in the United States of America

10 9 8 7 6 5 4 3 2 1

ISBN: 0-13-487935-X 01

Prentice-Hall International (UK) Limited, *London*
Prentice-Hall of Australia Pty. Limited, *Sydney*
Prentice-Hall Canada Inc., *Toronto*
Prentice-Hall Hispanoamericana, S.A., *Mexico*
Prentice-Hall of India Private Limited, *New Delhi*
Prentice-Hall of Japan, Inc., *Tokyo*
Prentice-Hall of Southeast Asia Pte. Ltd., *Singapore*
Editora Prentice-Hall do Brasil, Ltda., *Rio de Janeiro*

CONTENTS

TO THE STUDENT

This student guide is designed for use with the seventh edition of *Introduction to Management Accounting* by Charles T. Horngren and Gary L. Sundem. For each textbook chapter there is a corresponding guide chapter that presents the main focus and objectives and contains a detailed review of key ideas, plus a comprehensive set of practice test questions and problems. The solutions, which appear immediately after each practice test, can provide useful feedback to reinforce your learning.

HOW TO USE YOUR TEXTBOOK AND STUDENT GUIDE

Have you already developed a general study system or learning style that is most effective for you? Whether your answer is yes or no, please consider some time-tested ideas and procedures for the successful use of these materials in the study of management accounting.

1. First, don't assume that this study requires no more than the mere memorization of a few rules and definitions. Actually, it is essential that you develop for each chapter a clear understanding of the main concepts and their logical relationships. Remember that many of the chapters depend heavily on the earlier chapters in the textbook.

2. Don't try to digest an entire assignment in one long study session. This approach can be tiring, frustrating, and ineffective—or at least an inefficient way to use your time. Instead, profitably divide your study time into several shorter periods:
   (a) If an entire textbook chapter has been assigned for a class meeting, you may want, first, to read the chapter from beginning to end without interruption. Next, study the chapter in detail.
   (b) During this second study, carefully proceed through each step of all the examples and illustrations. Note particularly the "Summary Problems for Your Review." These cover the most important ideas in the chapter. Conscientiously trace each step in these problems to their solutions until your understanding is complete.

3. After your textbook study of a chapter, read the corresponding chapter in this student guide:
   (a) The "Review of Key Ideas" is a descriptive outline that can aid your retention of the most important concepts and relationships presented by the textbook chapter.
   (b) Solve the "Practice Test Questions and Problems." By checking your answers with the solutions, you can generate valuable feedback for mastering the chapter contents. At this point, don't hesitate to refer to your textbook as needed for more complete understanding.

4. Next, solve the textbook problems that have been assigned as homework by your instructor. Work alone, at least initially, and *not* with a "study buddy." Try to develop reliance on yourself, not on somebody else.

5. After the class discussion of the assigned problems, you can decide whether to restudy selected parts of the textbook.

REVIEWING FOR TESTS AND EXAMS

1. If you have regularly completed all of your study and written assignments on time, the necessary review for an exam will probably be *minimal*. In any case, you will find it infeasible to cover everything in detail. *Be selective.* Concentrate your review on either the most important matters or the textbook sections that seem most difficult for you.

2. You may find it helpful to "top off" your review by rereading selected parts of the student guide and reworking some of the practice test questions and problems.

Good luck!

Dudley W. Curry
Southern Methodist University

STUDENT GUIDE

Introduction to
MANAGEMENT
ACCOUNTING

PERSPECTIVE: SCOREKEEPING, ATTENTION DIRECTING, AND PROBLEM SOLVING

MAIN FOCUS AND OBJECTIVES

This preview chapter emphasizes the intertwining roles of managers and accountants in planning and controlling the operations of an organization. Our broad aim is to understand how accounting systems can aid *management decisions*.

Specific learning targets for this chapter are the meanings of some basic ideas:

- *Management functions*
- *Types of accounting data*
- *Line and staff authority*
- *Roles of accountants and treasurers*

The chapter presents the twin themes that permeate the field of management accounting: *the cost-benefit idea* and *the behavioral focus.*

REVIEW OF KEY IDEAS

A. Successful accounting systems provide information for three broad purposes or ends:
1. Reporting to managers for **planning and controlling routine operations.**
2. Reporting to managers for making special decisions and long-range plans, that is, for **strategic planning purposes.**
3. Reporting to stockholders, creditors, government agencies, and other outside parties.

B. Note how the primary targets of these purposes or ends are different:
1. The first two purposes deal with the **internal use** of information by managers: **management accounting.**
2. The third purpose is concerned mainly with the **external use** of information by investors: **financial accounting.**

C. Accounting systems produce three kinds of information:
   1. **Scorekeeping information** helps in the routine evaluation of performance and position.
   2. **Attention-directing information** aids in identifying problems and opportunities worth further investigation.
   3. **Problem-solving information** is useful for long-range planning and for making special, nonrecurring decisions.

D. Note the relationship between the management process and the internal accounting system.

> **See textbook Exhibit 1-2**

   1. **Decision making** is the nucleus of the management process and underlies two basic functions:
      a. **Planning:** deciding on objectives and means for their attainment.
      b. **Controlling:** consisting of evaluation through **feedback,** modification of plans, and actions to implement plans.
   2. The planning function is served mainly by **budgets.**
   3. The controlling function is served mainly by **performance reports.**
   4. The feedback loop in the diagram indicates the **interdependent nature** of planning and control.

E. **Feedback** is provided by performance reports that periodically compare actual operations with budget forecasts and show the amounts and explanations of variances.

> **See textbook Exhibits 1-3, 1-4, and 1-5**

   1. **Management by exception** means the concentration of executive attention and effort on the significant deviations from expected results.

> **Question: Does accounting do the controlling?**
> **Answer: No. See below.**

   2. Controlling consists of actions performed by **managers** and the evaluation that follows actions.
   3. Accounting **assists** the managerial control function by providing prompt measurements and by systematically identifying trouble spots.

F. The basic ideas of management accounting apply to service organizations as well as to manufacturing organizations.
   1. Service organizations produce a service instead of a tangible product.
      a. They include banks, insurance companies, railroads, theaters, and medical clinics.
      b. Nearly all nonprofit organizations are engaged in service activities—for example, universities, public libraries, churches, charitable organizations, and government agencies.
   2. What are the main distinctive characteristics of service organizations?
      a. They are **labor-intensive** and not capital-intensive.
      b. Their outputs are **difficult to define and measure.**
      c. Their major inputs and outputs are **intangible** and therefore **cannot be stored.**

G. The chief accounting executive, or chief management accountant, is often called the **controller.**

> **See textbook Exhibit 1-6**

1. The controller's authority is basically of the **staff type,** that is, giving advice and service to other departments.
2. The controller has direct control, called **line authority,** only over personnel of the controller's department, such as internal auditors, cost clerks, and the general ledger bookkeeper as shown in textbook Exhibit 1-7.
3. The main functions of the controller are planning, reporting, interpreting, evaluating, and consulting.
4. In contrast to the controller's functions, the **treasurer** of a company is concerned mainly with such financial activities as banking, short-term borrowing, and credits and collections.

H. Two major themes permeate the design of modern control systems:
1. **The cost-benefit theme:**
   a. All accounting systems and methods are economic goods available at various prices (**costs**).
   b. Such costs must be measured against the expected **benefits** of using particular ways to produce information for decision making.
   c. This means that it may often be more economical to gather desired data by one-time special efforts than by having a comprehensive system continuously gathering data that are seldom used.
2. **Behavioral implications:**
   a. Planning activities are emphasized by the use of budgets.
   b. Individual incentives are strongly influenced by performance reports that are used to appraise decisions, subunits, and managers.

I. Accounting activities can be divided into two broad areas: **management accounting** and **financial accounting.**

> **Question: Which two principal features of management accounting distinguish it from financial accounting?**
> **Answer: Internal orientation and freedom of choice. See below.**

1. Management accounting emphasizes the preparation of reports for **internal users** instead of the **external users** aimed at by financial accounting reports.
2. There is a greater **freedom of choice** in the measurements that may be made by management accounting systems.
   a. The measurements that can be reported by financial accounting systems are restricted by **generally accepted accounting principles (GAAP),** which are monitored by various public and private regulatory agencies.
   b. However, the only restrictions on measurements to be reported by management accounting systems are those that would be imposed by using the **cost-benefit philosophy.**

J. In comparison with financial accounting, the field of management accounting also emphasizes five other important ideas:

1. More concern for the **behavioral impact** of measurements and reports.
2. Greater emphasis on **future measurements.**
3. Use of **more flexible time spans** for reports.
4. Reporting of **more detail for subunits** of an organization.
5. Heavier **use of related disciplines,** e.g., economics, decision science.

K. Despite the greater freedom of choice permitted in management accounting systems, government regulations do have an important impact on internal accounting:
   1. Entities with government contracts must follow specified methods for determining contract costs for reimbursement purposes.
   2. The U.S. Foreign Corrupt Practices Act of 1977 imposes on all publicly held American companies several important responsibilities, including:
      a. Maintaining **appropriate internal accounting controls,** with mandatory documentation.
      b. Conducting **management audits** to verify implementation of stated opening policies.

L. Attractive aspects of management accounting education and practice include:
   1. ''Fast track to the top'' for business executives.
   2. Professional recognition as a Certified Management Accountant (CMA).

PRACTICE TEST QUESTIONS AND PROBLEMS WITH SOLUTIONS

I For each of the following multiple-choice and true-false statements, select the most appropriate answer and enter its identification letter in the space provided:

___ 1. Management accounting is the process of measuring and accumulating operating data of an organization for the decision purposes of stockholders, creditors, and other outside parties: (a) true, (b) false.

___ 2. Scorekeeping is the accumulation of data for use by: (a) bookkeepers, (b) internal managers, (c) external investors, (d) both internal managers and external investors.

___ 3. Preparing a monthly schedule of dollar sales by type of product and by name of salesperson is essentially: (a) a problem solving function, (b) an attention directing function, (c) a scorekeeping function.

___ 4. Management control refers primarily to the setting of maximum limits on expenditures: (a) true, (b) false.

___ 5. The management controlling function includes: (a) actions to carry out plans, (b) evaluation of results, (c) both of these, (d) neither of these.

___ 6. Budgets primarily serve: (a) the planning function, (b) the controlling function.

___ 7. Performance reports primarily serve: (a) the planning function, (b) the controlling function.

___ 8. Feedback is essential to: (a) management planning, (b) implementing plans, (c) evaluating actions, (d) all of these, (e) none of these.

___ 9. Controlling is done by: (a) accounting, (b) management, (c) both of these, (d) neither of these.

___ 10. Examples of service organizations include: (a) fireworks manufacturers, (b) self-service gasoline stations, (c) both of these, (d) neither of these.

___ 11. The controller's authority is basically of the: (a) staff type, (b) line type.

___ 12. The controller has direct authority over: (a) line departments, (b) members of the accounting department, (c) both of these, (d) neither of these.

___ 13. The controller is likened most aptly to the ship's: (a) captain, (b) engineer, (c) cook, (d) navigator, (e) executive officer.

___ 14. The treasurer of a company is concerned mainly with planning, reporting, interpreting, and consulting: (a) true, (b) false.

___ 15. The effective restrictions on measurements that can be reported by a management accounting system include: (a) generally accepted financial accounting standards, (b) the cost-benefit philosophy, (c) both of these, (d) neither of these.

___ 16. The behavioral implications of decisions and their implementation should usually be of concern to: (a) managers, (b) management accountants, (c) both of these, (d) neither of these.

___ 17. In the area of management accounting, the evaluation of performance should be made by comparing actual results for a period with: (a) the budget for the period, (b) actual results of the preceding period.

___ 18. Compared with the typical financial accounting reports, management accounting reports are more likely to deal with greater detail and for shorter time spans: (a) true, (b) false.

___ 19. Compared with the typical management accounting practice, the practice of financial accounting is more likely to make use of: (a) the decision sciences, (b) the behavioral sciences, (c) both of these, (d) neither of these.

___ 20. The practice of management accounting is not affected by government regulation: (a) true, (b) false.

___ 21. The U.S. Foreign Corrupt Practices Act of 1977 affects the operations of publicly held American companies that do all their business within the U.S.: (a) true, (b) false.

___ 22. Mandatory documentation of internal

controls by management is specified by GAAP: (a) true, (b) false.

___ 23. The primary responsibility of internal auditing staffs for conducting management audits is specified by: (a) GAAP, (b) Foreign Corrupt Practices Act, (c) both of these, (d) neither of these.

II Complete each of the following statements:

1. The three broad purposes or ends of successful accounting systems are:

(a) _____

_____

(b) _____

_____

(c) _____

_____

2. The three main types of useful information that the management accountant should supply are:

_____-keeping information,

_____-directing information, and

_____-solving information.

3. The two basic functions of the management process are _____ and

_____ .

4. Management planning is deciding on _____

_____ and _____

_____ .

5. The concentration of the executive's attention and effort on significant deviations from expected results is called _____ .

6. The three distinctive features of service organizations are:

(a) _____

_____

(b) _____

_____

(c) _____

_____

7. The chief accounting executive, or chief management accountant, is often called the _____ _____ .

8. Management accounting, in contrast to financial accounting, involves more emphasis on _____ use of data, _____ in choosing how measurements are to be made, and _____ considerations.

9. Write out in full the words for each of the following initials:

(a) GAAP: _____

_____

(b) CMA: _____

_____

(c) AICPA: _____

_____

(d) NAA: _____

_____

III For each of the following activities within a company, identify the main function that is being performed:

  PS: problem solving
  AD: attention directing
  SK: scorekeeping

____ 1. Analyzing deviations from the budget of the cost of materials used in making a certain product.

____ 2. Estimating future cash inflows and cash outflows relating to the contemplated acquisition of specialized manufacturing machinery.

____ 3. Computing and recording end-of-year adjustments for accrued wages and salaries.

____ 4. Tabulating spoiled rejected product units at the end of a manufacturing process.

____ 5. Entering checks in the cash disbursements journal.

IV Identify each of the following features as being primarily identified with management accounting (MA) or with financial accounting (FA):

____ 1. Less freedom in choosing measurement methods and principles.

____ 2. More detailed reports on subunits of an organization.

____ 3. Heavier use of the decision sciences.

____ 4. Stronger orientation to company creditors

____ 5. Heavier use of economics.

____ 6. Constrained by GAAP.

____ 7. Measuring actual performance against actual results of preceding period.

____ 8. Concerned primarily with impact on human behavior.

V For each of the following pairs, use the code shown below to indicate the usual type of authority of the first-named party over the second-named party:

  L: line authority
  S: staff authority
  N: no authority

____ 1. controller
    production superintendent

____ 2. president
    chairman of the board

____ 3. chief inspector
    controller

____ 4. controller
    payroll clerks

____ 5. production superintendent
    accounts payable bookkeeper

____ 6. engineering vice-president
    storekeeper

___ 7. manufacturing vice-president
receiving clerk

___ 8. assistant controller
accounts receivable bookkeeper

___ 9. controller
purchasing officer

___ 10. internal auditor
assistant controller

VI For each of the following employees of a company, use the code below to indicate the major type of duty that would usually be performed:

SK: scorekeeping
AD: attention directing
PS: problem solving

___ 1. cost analyst

___ 2. head of internal auditing

___ 3. head of special reports and studies

___ 4. accounts receivable clerk

___ 5. payroll clerk

CHAPTER 1 SOLUTIONS TO PRACTICE TEST QUESTIONS AND PROBLEMS

I

1 b	4 b	7 b	10 d	13 d	16 c	19 d	22 b
2 d	5 c	8 d	11 a	14 b	17 a	20 b	23 b
3 b	6 a	9 b	12 b	15 b	18 a	21 a	

II   1 (a) internal planning and controlling routine operations, (b) internal strategic planning purposes, and (c) external reporting to stockholders and others, 2 scorekeeping information, attention-directing information, and problem-solving information, 3 planning and controlling, 4 objectives and ways to achieve them, 5 management by exception, 6 (a) highest costs are related to payroll (labor is intensive), (b) output is hard to define and measure, (c) major inputs and outputs cannot be stored, 7 controller, 8 internal use of data, freedom in choosing how measurements are to be made, behavioral considerations, 9 (a) Generally Accepted Accounting Principles, (b) Certified Management Accountant, (c) American Institute of Certified Public Accountants, (d) National Association of Accountants.

III   1 AD   2 PS   3 SK   4 SK   5 SK

IV   1 FA   2 MA   3 MA   4 FA   5 MA   6 FA   7 FA   8 MA

V   1 S   2 N   3 N   4 L   5 N   6 N   7 L   8 L   9 S   10 N

VI   1 AD   2 AD   3 PS   4 SK   5 SK

INTRODUCTION TO
COST-VOLUME RELATIONSHIPS

MAIN FOCUS AND OBJECTIVES

This chapter presents a powerful prediction model to assist planning decisions. It is called *cost-volume-profit analysis* or *breakeven analysis*. The overriding concept is:

Contribution Margin = Sales − Variable Costs

To use this concept, you must have a clear understanding of:

- *The distinction between variable costs and fixed costs*
- *The meaning of relevant range*

Be sure that, through practice in solving problems, you attain a comfortable ability level in using the two methods for making a cost-volume-profit analysis: the *contribution-margin technique* and the *equation technique*.

REVIEW OF KEY IDEAS

A. Suppose a shoe company increases its level or volume of activity (shoes produced or labor hours worked, etc.).

    1. Question: How are fixed costs and variable costs affected?

        Answer: *(within Relevant Range)*

change in total as vol. changes/no change unit cost

total stay same as vol changes, but unit cost changes

Cost Type	Total Cost	Unit Cost
Variable	Increase	No Change
Fixed	No Change	Decrease

sales comm., materials, parts

rent, execu salaries

    2. The logic that supports these answers is tied directly to the definitions of these two main types of costs:

3. **Variable costs** are costs that **change in total** in direct proportion to changes in volume of activity.
   a. Therefore, variable costs **stay the same per unit of activity.**

> **See textbook Exhibit 2-1**

---

   b. Examples of variable cost include sales commissions and most kinds of merchandise, materials, and parts.
4. **Fixed costs** are the costs that **stay the same in total** over a wide range of activity volume.
   a. Therefore, fixed costs **do not stay the same per unit of activity** of different volume levels; fixed costs on a per-unit basis vary **inversely** with changes in activity volume.

> **Why?**
> **Answer: Assume that volume increases. There will be more units over which to spread the same total fixed costs. For example, if the shoe company has $1 million of fixed costs to make 100,000 pairs of shoes, cost per pair is $1,000,000 ÷ 100,000 = $10. Next year, if 200,000 pairs are made with no change in total fixed costs, cost per pair is reduced to $1,000,000 ÷ 200,000 = $5. Thus, when volume increased, fixed costs on a per-unit basis decreased.**

   b. Examples of fixed-cost items include factory rent, executive salaries, and straight-line depreciation.
   c. A cost is fixed only in relationship to a given planning period for the expected band of activity volume, which is called the **relevant range.**
   d. Activity volume beyond either side of this range would require major adjustments in operations that would have basic effects on fixed costs.

> **See textbook Exhibit 2-2**

---

   e. Activity outside the relevant range could also affect the **variable cost per unit of activity.**
5. Costs do not necessarily behave in a **linear** manner, and therefore we cannot always classify them into perfectly variable and perfectly fixed categories.
   a. Some costs may be **nonlinear** because they are affected simultaneously by **several different** activity bases.
   b. Usually, however, we associate a given variable cost with **only one** measure of volume, and that relationship is assumed to be **linear,** for example, pairs of shoes manufactured.

B. Management planning decisions are often facilitated by an analysis of the cost-volume-profit relationships and the effects on net income of each of several alternative combinations of product selling prices, variable costs per unit, and total fixed costs. This approach is often called **break-even analysis,** although a more appropriate term is **cost-volume-profit analysis.**

1. The **break-even point** is that point of activity (level of sales volume) where total expenses equal total revenues. At this point there is zero net income.
2. **Contribution margin** is the excess of sales over variable costs, and it can be expressed as total dollars, dollars per product unit, percentage of sales, or ratio to sales.
   a. Example: selling price $5, variable cost per unit $2, total fixed costs $600.
   b. Contribution margin **per unit** is $5 − $2 = $3
   c. Contribution-margin **ratio** is $3 ÷ $5 = 60% = .6
3. **Contribution-margin technique** for computing breakeven point:
   a. Formula:

$$\text{Break-even point} = \frac{\text{Fixed expenses}}{\text{Contribution margin}}$$

   b. Break-even point in terms of **product units:** divide total fixed expenses by **contribution margin per unit:**

$$\frac{\$600}{\$3} = 200 \text{ units}$$

   c. Break-even point in terms of **total dollar sales:** divide total fixed expenses by **contribution-margin ratio** or **percentage of sales:**

$$\frac{\$600}{.6} = \$1,000$$

   d. Prove these answers by filling these blanks:

Sales (_____ units × $ _____) =		$ _____
Less expenses:		
Variable (_____ units × $ _____) =	$ _____	
Fixed	$ _____	$ _____
Net income		$ _-0-_

3. The **equation technique** of determining the break-even point is based on the fundamental relationships among the principal elements of the income statement:
   a.

Sales		XXX
Less:		
Variable expenses	XXX	
Fixed expenses	XXX	XXX
Net income		XXX

   b. The equation form of this income statement is:

$$\text{Sales} - \text{Variable Expenses} - \text{Fixed Expenses} = \text{Net Income}$$

   c. **Example:** selling price $5, variable cost per unit $2, total fixed costs $600, break-even units X, net income zero:

$$\$5X - \$2X - \$600 = 0$$
$$\$3X = \$600$$
$$X = \frac{\$600}{\$3} = 200 \text{ units}$$

   d. The break-even point in total dollar sales for this example is 200 units times $5 = $1,000.
4. Instead of using the equation method, you can often find the break-even point more quickly and more easily by using the contribution-margin technique.

5. Note well that the contribution-margin technique is merely the final step by the equation technique.
6. The sales in terms of total sales dollars or product units that must be made to attain a certain **target net income** can be computed simply:

$$\frac{\text{Fixed Expenses} + \text{Target Net Income}}{\text{Contribution-Margin Ratio or Per Unit}}$$

7. The **graphical technique** is useful in portraying the concept of break-even analysis and the relationships among costs, volume, and profit.

> See textbook Exhibit 2-3

   a. This technique can effectively portray profit potentials over a wide range of volume.
   b. When operating budgets are being considered, break-even graphs can improve management's understanding of budget relationships and effects.

C. Cost-volume-profit analysis helps to focus management's efforts on obtaining an optimal combination of product selling prices, variable costs per unit, and total fixed costs.
   1. The most desirable combinations would have **both** low fixed costs and large contributing margins.
   2. However, it is often necessary in practice to make a **trade-off** (strike a balance) between fixed costs and contribution margins.

D. In break-even analysis, accountants usually assume **linear relationships**—over the relevant range—between expenses and activity volume and between revenues and activity volume. More specifically, the following assumptions are commonly made, and they must be clearly recognized as limitations to the use of break-even analysis:
   1. Unit selling prices and unit variable costs are constant at different activity levels.
   2. All costs are divisible into the strictly fixed and variable elements described in this chapter.
   3. No changes in efficiency and productivity occur at different volume levels.
   4. There will be a constant **sales mix**, the relative combination of a variety of company products that make up total sales.
   5. There will be a negligible difference between inventory levels at the beginning and end of a period.

E. Do not confuse contribution margin with gross margin.
   1. **Contribution margin** is the excess of sales over **total variable costs,** including both variable cost of goods sold and variable operating expenses, if any.
   2. **Gross margin** (or **gross profit**) is the excess of sales over **total cost of goods sold,** including both variable cost of goods sold and fixed cost of goods sold, if any.

PRACTICE TEST QUESTIONS AND PROBLEMS WITH SOLUTIONS

I For each of the following multiple-choice and true-false statements, select the most appropriate answer and enter its identification letter in the space provided:

____ 1. Variable costs on a per-unit basis tend to vary inversely with changes in activity volume: (a) true, (b) false.

____ 2. Total fixed costs are $30,000 when 10,000 product units are produced. When 15,000 units are produced, fixed costs would tend to be: (a) $45,000 in total, (b) $3.00 per unit, (c) $20,000 in total, (d) $2.00 per unit.

____ 3. When manufacturing volume decreases, fixed costs will be: (a) more per product unit, (b) the same per product unit, (c) less per product unit.

____ 4. Over the relevant range of activity, variable costs stay the same per unit of activity: (a) true, (b) false.

____ 5. We usually assume that a given variable cost: (a) is associated with only one measure of volume, (b) has a linear relationship with volume, (c) both of these, (d) neither of these.

____ 6. Total variable costs are $60,000 when 15,000 product units are produced. When 20,000 units are produced, variable costs would tend to be: (a) $3.00 per unit, (b) $60,000 in total, (c), $4.00 per unit, (d) $40,000 in total.

____ 7. See the preceding test item. If all units are sold for $10 each, the contribution margin would be: (a) $4.00 per unit, (b) $100,000, (c) 60%, (d) 40%.

____ 8. The break-even point is usually measured in terms of: (a) number of employees, (b) product selling prices, (c) units or dollars of sales, (d) capital invested or size of company.

____ 9. The break-even point can be determined simply by measuring the fixed and variable expenses in a given income statement and finding their total: (a) true, (b) false.

____ 10. Monthly production of a company consists of 2,000 units sold at $5.00 per unit. Total costs are $4,200 fixed and $4,000 variable. The break-even point per month is: (a) 2,000 units, (b) 1,800 units, (c) 1,600 units, (d) 1,400 units.

____ 11. Monthly sales of a company are $16,000 with total costs of $6,000 fixed and $8,000 variable. The break-even point per month is total sales of: (a) $16,000, (b) $14,000, (c) $12,000, (d) $10.000.

____ 12. In the usual break-even graph, activity

volume in units is measured on the: (a) vertical scale or axis, (b) horizontal scale or axis.

____ 13. The number of product units that must be sold to earn a specified amount of net income can be computed by dividing the unit contribution margin into the sum of fixed expenses and target net income: (a) true, (b) false.

____ 14. A company produces a product for sale at $24 per unit. Costs are $48,000 per month for total fixed costs and $16 for variable costs per unit. Compute the monthly break-even point in units: (a) 7,500, (b) 6,000, (c) 3,750, (d) 3,000.

____ 15. See the preceding test item. The number of units to be produced and sold per month at the same $24 price to obtain a profit of $12,000 per month would be: (a) 7,500, (b) 6,000, (c) 3,750, (d) 3,000.

____ 16. Monthly sales for a certain product are $8,000 with total fixed costs of $2,000 and total variable costs of $4,000. Compute the monthly break-even point: (a) $4,000, (b) $5,000, (c) $6,000, (d) $7,000.

____ 17. See the preceding test item. Sales per month to produce a $1,000 profit would be: (a) $4,000, (b) $5,000, (c) $6,000, (d) $7,000.

____ 18. As sales exceed the break-even point, a small contribution-margin ratio would result in less additional profit than would a large contribution-margin ratio: (a) true, (b) false.

____ 19. If the total contribution margin in a given case increased by a certain total amount, net income would: (a) increase by the same amount, (b) decrease by the same amount, (c) be unaffected.

____ 20. The break-even point would be decreased by: (a) a decrease in fixed costs, (b) an increase in the contribution-margin ratio, (c) a decrease in the ratio of variable costs to sales, (d) all of these, (e) none of these.

____ 21. The linearity assumption for break-even graphs is likely to be most accurate: (a) below the relevant range of volume, (b) within the relevant range of volume, (c) above the relevant range of volume.

___ 22. One of the several assumptions underlying typical break-even charts is that changes in efficiency and productivity occur at different levels: (a) true, (b) false.

___ 23. The conventional break-even chart is based upon assumptions that include unchanging amounts for selling prices, unit variable costs, and total fixed costs: (a) true, (b) false.

___ 24. Gross margin is sales minus: (a) all variable costs, (b) cost of goods sold, including both variable and fixed elements.

___ 25. Given for Cisneros Co. (in thousands): sales $80, manufacturing costs $32 (half variable), and operating expenses $40 (75% fixed). Ignore inventories and compute gross margin: (a) $40, (b) $64, (c) $34, (d) none of these.

___ 26. See the preceding test item and compute contribution margin: (a) $48, (b) $54, (c) $38, (d) none of these.

Appendix 2A

___ 27. A company produces and sells two products at contribution margins of $2 for X and $5 for Y. Fixed costs are $10,500. If the planned mix is five units of X for each unit of Y, the break-even point in terms of **total** units would be: (a) 1,800, (b) 4,200, (c) 9,000, (d) some other number.

Appendix 2B

___ 28. A company produces a product for sale at $24 per unit. Costs are $48,000 for total fixed costs and $16.00 for variable costs per unit. The number of units to be produced and sold to obtain a $4,800 profit after income taxes of 60% would be: (a) 3,000, (b) 3,750, (c) 6,000, (d) 7,500.

II Complete each of the following statements:

1. The wide span of activity over which certain costs are fixed is called _____.

2. As production volume decreases, _____ costs become larger on a per-unit basis.

3. Contribution margin is defined as _____ minus _____.

4. The most desirable combination of fixed costs and contribution margins would include high _____ and low _____.

5. The typical break-even graph shows a _____ _____ type of behavior for expenses and revenues over the relevant range.

6. A decrease in total fixed costs in a given case would cause the break-even point to _____.

III All of these data pertain to the monthly production and sales of Dauphin Company. Fill the blanks, assuming that all costs and expenses are divided into strictly fixed and strictly variable elements.

Activity Volume	Total Fixed Costs	Total Variable Costs	Fixed Costs per Unit	Variable Costs per Unit
10,000	$36,000	$35,000	$ _____(1)	$ _____(2)
12,000	$ _____(3)	$ _____(4)	$ _____(5)	$ _____(6)
8,000	$ _____(7)	$ _____(8)	$ _____(9)	$ _____(10)

IV 1. Using the data given below, construct a cost-volume-profit graph in the format of the textbook Exhibit 2-3:

Sales, 1,000 units at $10 each
Variable expenses, $6 per unit
Fixed expenses: $2,000

2. What is the break-even point?

(a) In units: _____

(b) In total sales dollars: _____

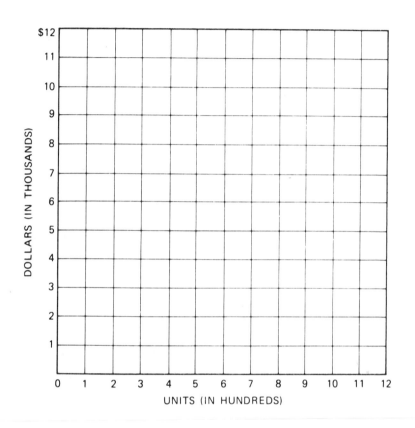

V Given for one of the products of Chavez Co:

Sales price per product unit $40
Variable expenses per product unit $25
Total fixed expenses $30,000

Find:
1. Contribution margin per product unit .... $ _____

2. Break-even sales in units .... _____ units

3. Sales in units that will produce a net income of $6,000 .... _____ units

4. Sales in units that will produce a net income of 25% of sales .... _____ units

5. Net income if 3,200 product units are sold .... $ _____

6. The break-even sales in units if variable expenses are increased by $3 per unit
   and if total fixed expenses are decreased by $9,000. .... _____ units

7. If the company desires a net income of $15,000 on a sales volume of
   5,000 units, what must the unit selling price be, assuming no changes in the
   $25 variable expenses per unit or the $30,000 total fixed expenses? .... $ _____

VI   Given for Comini Corporation:

Sales	$50,000
Total fixed expenses	$12,000
Total variable expenses	$35,000

Find:

1. Variable-cost ratio .... _____ %

2. Contribution-margin ratio .... _____ %

3. Break-even sales .... $ _____

4. Sales that would produce a net income of $9,000, assuming no change in
   the variable-cost ratio or the total fixed expenses .... $ _____

5. Sales that would provide a net income of 10% of sales, assuming no change
   in the variable-cost ratio or the total fixed expenses .... $ _____

6. Break-even sales if total fixed expenses are reduced by $3,000 and if selling
   prices are reduced by 20% per product unit, assuming no change in the ratio
   of variable costs to the number of product units produced and sold .... $ _____

VII Nandi Products, Inc. produces and sells two products as follows:

	Q	P
Selling prices per unit	$25	$18
Variable costs per unit	20	15

Total fixed costs are $15,750.

Compute the break-even point in terms of **total** units for each of these planned mixes:

1. Three Q's for each P .... _____ units

2. Three P's for each Q .... _____ units

Appendix 2B

VIII Given for Grossinger, Inc.:

Product selling price per unit	$20
Variable expenses per unit	$14
Fixed expenses	$10,000
Target profit after taxes	$ 2,000
Income tax rate	60%

Compute the number of product units that must be sold to achieve the target profit after taxes.

CHAPTER 2 SOLUTIONS TO PRACTICE TEST QUESTIONS AND PROBLEMS

I

1 b	5 c	9 b	13 a	17 c	21 b	25 d
2 d	6 c	10 d	14 b	18 a	22 b	26 b
3 a	7 c	11 c	15 a	19 a	23 a	27 b
4 a	8 c	12 b	16 a	20 d	24 b	28 d

Computations:

2 $30,000 ÷ 15,000 = $2.00 (d)

6 $60,000 ÷ 15,000 = $4.00 (c)

7 Variable cost per unit is $60,000 ÷ 15,000 = $4;
contribution margin per unit is $10 − $4 = $6;
contribution-margin ratio is $6 ÷ $10 = 60% (c)

10 $4,000 ÷ 2,000 = $2; $5 − $2 = $3 contribution margin; $4,200 ÷ $3 = 1,400 units (d)

11 $16,000 − $8,000 = $8,000; $8,000 ÷ $16,000 = 50% contribution margin; $6,000 ÷ 50% = $12,000 (c)

14 $48,000 ÷ ($24 − $16) = $48,000 ÷ $8 = 6,000 units (b)

15 $24 − $16 = $8 contribution margin;
($48,000 + $12,000) ÷ $8 = $60,000 ÷ $8 = 7,500 units (a)

16 ($8,000 − $4,000) ÷ $8,000 = $50%; $2,000 ÷ 50% = $4,000 (a)

17 $8,000 − $4,000 = $4,000; $4,000 ÷ $8,000 = 50% contribution margin;
($2,000 + $1,000) ÷ 50% = $3,000 ÷ 50% = $6,000 (c)

25 $80 − $32 = $48 (d)

26 $80 − ($32 × .5) − ($40 × .25) = $80 − $16 − $10 = $54 (b)

27 (5 × $2) + $5 = $15; $15 ÷ (5 + 1) = $2.50 average contribution margin per unit;
$10,500 ÷ $2.50 = 4,200 total units (b)

28 $4,800 ÷ (1 − 60%) = $4,800 ÷ 40% = $12,000 profit before 60% income taxes;
$24 − $16 = $8; ($48,000 + $12,000) ÷ $8 = $60,000 ÷ $8 = 7,500 units (d)

II   1 the relevant range, 2 fixed, 3 total sales (or selling price per unit) minus total variable costs (or variable costs per unit), 4 high unit contribution margins and low total fixed costs, 5 a linear (or straight-line), 6 decrease.

III   Dauphin Company

1 $3.60	3 $36,000	5 $3.00	7 $36,000	9 $4.50
2 $3.50	4 $42,000	6 $3.50	8 $28,000	10 $3.50

Computations:

1 $36,000 ÷ 10,000 = $3.60

2 $35,000 ÷ 10,000 = $3.50

4 $35,000 (12,000 ÷ 10,000) = $35,000 × 120% = $42,000

5 $36,000 ÷ 12,000 = $3.00

8 $35,000 (8,000 ÷ 10,000) = $35,000 × 80% = $28,000

9 $36,000 ÷ 8,000 = $4.50

IV   Cost-Volume-Profit Graph

Break-even point can also be computed: fixed expenses divided by contribution margin per unit; $2,000 ÷ ($10 − $6) = $2,000 ÷ $4 = 500 units, or $5,000 at a $10 selling price per unit.

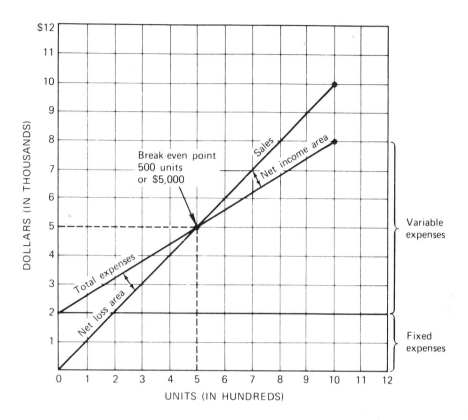

V   Chavez Co.

1. Unit contribution margin is unit selling price less unit variable expenses: 40 − 25 = $15.
2. Break-even sales in units is total fixed expenses divided by unit contribution margin: 30,000 ÷ 15 = 2,000 units.
3. Unit sales to produce a target net income would be the sum of the total fixed expenses and the target net income divided by the unit combination margin:
   (30,000 + 6,000) ÷ 15 = 36,000 ÷ 15 = 2,400 units.
4. If the target net income is 25% of sales, the target net income per product unit would be (25%) (40) = $10 per unit. Therefore the dollars per product unit available for coverage of the total fixed expenses would be the unit sales price less the unit net income less the unit variable costs: 40 − 10 − 25 = $5 per unit. Dividing this into the total fixed expenses gives us the required sales in units: 30,000 ÷ 5 = 6,000 units.
5. Each unit would contribute $15 toward total fixed expenses. Therefore net income would be: (15) (3,200) − 30,000 = 48,000 − 30,000 = $18,000.
6. The new unit contribution margin would be: 40 − (25 + 3) = $12 per unit. The new total fixed expenses would be: 30,000 − 9,000 = $21,000. Therefore the new break-even sales in units would be: 21,000 ÷ 12 = 1,750 units.
7. The necessary unit contribution to cover both the target net income and the total fixed expenses would be: (15,000 + 30,000) ÷ 5,000 = $9 per product unit. Therefore the selling price per unit would be the variable cost per unit plus this unit contribution margin: 25 + 9 = $34 per unit.

VI Comini Corporation

1. Variable-cost ratio is total variable expenses divided by sales:
   $35,000 \div 50,000 = 70\%$.
2. Contribution-margin ratio is the complement of the variable cost ratio:
   $100\% - 70\% = 30\%$; or $(50,000 - 35,000) \div 50,000 = 15,000 \div 50,000 = 30\%$.
3. Break-even sales are total fixed expenses divided by the contribution-margin ratio:
   $12,000 \div 30\% = 12,000 \div .30 = \$40,000$.
4. Divide the sum of the fixed expenses and the desired net income (target net income) by the contribution-margin ratio:
   $(12,000 + 9,000) \div 30\% = 21,000 \div .30 = \$70,000$.
5. These sales would be total fixed expenses divided by the excess of the contribution-margin ratio (or percent) over the net-income ratio (or percent):
   $12,000 \div (30\% - 10\%) = 12,000 \div 20\% = 12,000 \div .20 = \$60,000$.
   Another approach would be to set up an equation with S for the required sales and using the 70% variable-cost ratio and the 10% net-income ratio:
   $S = 12,000 + 70\%S + 10\%S = 12,000 + 80\%S$
   $20\%S = 12,000$
   $S = 12,000 \div 20\% = 12,000 \div .20 = \$60,000$.
6. The new total fixed expenses would be: $12,000 - 3,000 = \$9,000$. The new variable-cost ratio **(to total dollar sales)** would be:
   $35,000 \div (50,000 - 20\% \text{ of } 50,000) = 35,000 \div 40,000 = 7/8$, or 87 1/2%.
   Therefore the new contribution-margin ratio would be 1/8, or 12 1/2%. The new break-even sales would then be the new total fixed expenses divided by the new contribution-margin ratio:
   $9,000 \div 1/8 = (9,000)(8) = \$72,000$.

VII Nandi Products, Inc.

Contribution margins are $\$25 - \$20 = \$5$ for Q and $\$18 - \$15 = \$3$ for P.
1. $(3 \times \$5) + \$3 = \$18$; $\$18 \div (3 + 1) = \$4.50$ average contribution margin per unit; $\$15,750 \div \$4.50 = 3,500$ total units.
2. $(3 \times \$3) + \$5 = \$14$; $\$14 \div (3 + 1) = \$3.50$; $\$15,750 \div \$3.50 = 4,500$ total units.

VIII Grossinger, Inc.

Let X = number of units to be sold.
$$20X = 14X + 10,000 + \frac{2,000}{1 - .6}$$
$$6X = 10,000 + \frac{2,000}{.4}$$
$$6X = 10,000 + 5,000 = 15,000$$
$$X = 15,000 \div 6 = 2,500 \text{ units}$$

INTRODUCTION TO MANUFACTURING COSTS

MAIN FOCUS AND OBJECTIVES

We focus in this chapter on *manufacturing costs*, which usually mean the costs of producing tangible products. The basic elements of these costs are:

- *Direct materials*
- *Direct labor*
- *Factory overhead*

We seek to learn what these elements are, how they contrast to non-manufacturing costs, and how they relate to the balance sheet and income statement. Thus, we must grasp the essential distinction between two broad types of costs: *product costs* and *period costs*.

Another main learning objective is to understand how and why the income statements of manufacturing companies can be constructed by either of two ways: *the absorption approach* and *the contribution approach*.

REVIEW OF KEY IDEAS

A. Basic cost terms:
  1. **Cost:** the monetary measurement of an exchange of resources, for example, the dollars paid for paper or for typesetting labor by a newspaper publisher.
  2. **Expense:** a cost that is being deducted from (matched against) revenue in a given period, for example, salesmen's salaries.
  3. **Cost objective:** any activity for which a separate measurement of costs is desired, for example, the cost of operating the building maintenance department or the cost of producing pocket calculators by an electronics firm.
  4. A **cost accounting system** has two main elements:

> See textbook Exhibit 3-1

Something we want to know the cost of

      a. The **accumulation** of initial costs by such natural classes as material or labor.

      b. The **allocation** of these costs to cost objectives for purposes of evaluating the performance of manufacturing departments and measuring the costs of outputs (end products and services produced for customers).

  5. The terms **direct costs** and **indirect costs** refer to their relationships to a particular cost object.

      a. Essentially, the distinction between direct and indirect costs depends on the **closeness of their identification with the cost object.**

      b. In our book, unless otherwise stated, we take only the **product** cost objective as our focal point for identifying costs as direct or indirect.

      c. For example, although a foreman's salary may be **direct** in relation to the department that he has charge of, we will call it **indirect** (in relation to the different kinds of **products** processed through that department).

B. Basic elements of manufacturing cost:

  1. **Direct materials:** the acquisition cost of materials that are physically identifiable as part of the finished goods and can be traced to the finished goods in an economically feasible way; for example, fabrics, wood, and hardware used to make chairs by a furniture manufacturing company.

  2. **Direct labor:** the wages of labor that are physically traceable to the finished goods in an economically feasible way, for example, wages of product assemblers and machine operators in an appliance manufacturing company.

  3. **Factory overhead** includes all costs other than direct material and direct labor that are involved with manufacturing operations, for example, factory cleaning supplies consumed, indirect labor used, power costs, and depreciation of factory facilities.

      a. These are **indirect** manufacturing costs in relation to the products manufactured.

      b. Other terms used for factory overhead are **factory burden, manufacturing overhead, manufacturing expenses,** and **indirect manufacturing costs.**

C. Two main types of factory overhead:

  1. **Variable factory overhead** usually includes supplies and most indirect labor.

  2. **Fixed factory overhead** usually includes supervisory salaries, property taxes, rent, insurance, and depreciation.

D. Pairs of the major cost elements are sometimes combined in cost terminology as follows:

$$\textbf{PRIME COST} = \left\{ \begin{array}{|c|} \hline \textbf{Direct Materials} \\ \hline \textbf{Direct Labor} \\ \hline \textbf{Factory Overhead} \\ \hline \end{array} \right\} = \textbf{CONVERSION COST}$$

E. Can you distinguish between product costs and period costs?

See textbook Exhibit 3-3

  1. Note that **product costs** are identified with goods produced or purchased for resale; that is, they are **inventoriable.**

      a. Examples are direct materials, direct labor, and all kinds of factory overhead.

      b. Any unsold part of product costs is an **asset** in the form of inventory:
         Note the triple stages of inventory for a manufacturing company: direct material, work in process, and finished goods.

Note also that factory overhead cost is transformed into inventory assets along with direct materials and direct labor.

      c.   The sold part of product costs becomes an expense in the form of cost of goods sold.

  2. **Period costs** are costs that are deductible as expenses without going through an inventory stage.

      a.   Such costs are **not inventoriable** and should be entirely classified as expenses by both merchandisers and manufacturers.

      b.   These include principally the selling and administrative expenses, for example, salaries of salesmen and the credit manager, and depreciation of store equipment.

F.   The financial statements of merchandisers and manufacturers differ because of the types of goods they sell.

  1. **Merchandising companies** sell goods without changing their basic form.

      a.   Their balance sheets usually carry only one major type of inventory item, **merchandise.**

      b.   Their income statements report the cost of goods sold as the **purchase costs** of merchandise acquired and resold, including freight charges.

  2. **Manufacturing companies** transform materials into other goods through the use of labor and factory facilities.

      a.   Their balance sheets usually report three major types of inventory: **direct materials, work in process,** and **finished goods.**

      b.   Their income statements show the **manufacturing costs** of goods produced and sold.

See textbook Exhibit 3-4

Question: Can you construct such a model income statement with your textbook closed?

G.   Textbook Exhibit 3-5 is a simplified summary of the balance sheet equation:

Assets equal Equities

or

Assets equal Liabilities plus Stockholders' Equity

  1. Your careful analysis of this exhibit will help you link the meaningful concepts of this chapter with the more fundamental ideas of financial accounting.

  2. You should especially note the following:

      a.   How manufacturing costs are traced in three stages through the inventory accounts (assets) and finally to the cost of goods sold (expense).

      b.   How the cost of goods sold and other expenses are deducted from revenue to measure the net increase in the retained income portion of stockholders' equity.

H. There are two important forms of the income statement:

    1. The **absorption approach** is also referred to as **absorption costing, full costing, traditional costing,** or **functional costing.**

See textbook Exhibit 3-8

       a. All manufacturing costs, **including fixed factory overhead,** are considered to be inventoriable or product costs that do not become expenses until sales take place.

       b. Note that the absorption approach makes a primary classification of costs according to **manufacturing and nonmanufacturing functions,** emphasizing the **gross profit margin** available to cover selling and administrative expenses.

    2. The **contribution form** is also called **variable costing, direct costing,** or **marginal costing.**

See textbook Exhibit 3-9

       a. Only variable manufacturing costs **(excluding fixed factory overhead)** are considered to be inventoriable or product costs.

       b. Note that the contribution approach makes a primary classification of costs into **variable and fixed elements,** emphasizing the **contribution margin** available to cover the fixed costs.

    3. To summarize the difference between these two models of the income statement, the primary classification of costs is:

       a. **By management functions for the absorption form** and

       b. **By cost behavior patterns for the contribution form.**

Question: Can you construct model income statements using each of these approaches? See Practice Test Problem VI.

    4. In contrast to the traditional structure of the income statement, the measurement of contribution margins can provide important advantages to management, especially when reported by divisions and product lines.

       a. In general, the contribution approach facilitates cost-volume-profit analysis and helps management planning, as explained in the preceding chapter.

       b. More specifically, the management uses of the contribution approach are described in the next chapter.

PRACTICE TEST QUESTIONS AND PROBLEMS WITH SOLUTIONS

I For each of the following multiple-choice statements, select the most appropriate answer and enter its identification letter in the space provided:

_____ 1. Examples of direct labor cost for a manufacturer of oil well drilling tools would include: (a) salary of the plant superintendent, (b) salary of the sales manager, (c) wages of a secretary in the plant office, (d) none of these.

_____ 2. Examples of factory overhead cost would typically include: (a) wages of an assembly worker, (b) salary of the plant manager, (c) both of these, (d) neither of these.

3. Examples of direct material cost would usually include: (a) fuel for manufacturing, (b) abrasives for shaping products, (c) both of these, (d) neither of these.

4. Factory overhead costs usually include: (a) direct manufacturing costs, (b) indirect manufacturing costs, (c) both of these, (d) neither of these.

5. The wages of factory janitors and maintenance personnel would usually be classified as: (a) factory overhead cost, (b) direct labor cost, (c) nonmanufacturing cost, (d) none of these.

6. The three basic elements of manufacturing costs are direct labor, direct materials, and: (a) indirect manufacturing costs, (b) indirect materials, (c) indirect labor, (d) none of these.

7. The usual basis for distinction between direct and indirect costs is: (a) their relative size, (b) their relative frequency of occurrence, (c) their relation to the product, (d) none of these.

8. Conversion cost is direct labor plus: (a) direct material, (b) factory overhead, (c) selling and administrative expense, (d) all of these.

9. Prime cost minus conversion cost is equal to: (a) direct material cost, (b) direct labor cost minus conversion cost, (c) direct material cost minus factory overhead, (d) none of the above.

10. These amounts are included in the operating statement of a company: direct material costs $60,000, selling expenses $25,000, factory overhead $43,000, interest expense $6,000, direct labor $75,000, work-in-progress inventory $13,000. The prime cost is: (a) $178,000, (b) $118,000, (c) $209,000, (d) $135,000, (e) some other amount.

11. See the preceding test item. The conversion cost is: (a), (b), (c), (d), (e).

12. Product costs of a floor covering manufacturer would include: (a) direct material cost, (b) variable factory overhead, (c) both of these, (d) neither of these.

13. Product costs: (a) are inventoriable, (b) eventually become expenses, (c) both of these, (d) neither of these.

14. Period costs: (a) are inventoriable, (b) may be transformed into assets, (c) both of these, (d) neither of these.

15. Period costs should be entirely classified as expenses: (a) by manufacturers, (b) by merchandisers, (c) both of these, (d) neither of these.

16. Product costs would usually include: (a) fire insurance on factory machinery, (b) sales commissions, (c) both of these, (d) neither of these.

17. These amounts appear in the absorption form income statement of a company: depreciation of store building $4,200, fire insurance on work in process $1,500, lubricants used in manufacturing operations $2,500, legal expenses $3,000. The total product costs included above are: (a) $4,000, (b) $8,000, (c) $11,000, (d) $5,500, (e) $7,200.

18. See the preceding test item. The total period costs included are: (a), (b), (c), (d), (e).

19. Period costs would usually include: (a) depreciation of factory equipment, (b) depreciation of sales equipment, (c) both of these, (d) neither of these.

20. The cost of goods sold by a manufacturer would include some of the company's: (a) variable factory overhead cost, (b) direct labor cost, (c) both of these, (d) neither of these.

21. The current assets in the balance sheet of a merchandiser would include inventories of: (a) work in process, (b) direct materials, (c) both of these, (d) neither of these.

22. Given for Ken Co. (in thousands): sales $80, direct material $12, direct labor $22, selling and administrative expenses $15 (two-thirds fixed), factory overhead $24 (three-fourths fixed). Compute amount of gross profit: (a) $7, (b) $28, (c) $35, (d) none of these.

___ 23. See the preceding test item. Compute amount of contribution margin: (a) $22, (b) $47, (c) $35, (d) none of these.

___ 24. The contribution approach to income measurement makes a primary classification of costs according to: (a) manufacturing and nonmanufacturing functions, (b) fixed and variable cost elements.

___ 25. The absorption approach to income measurement emphasizes: (a) the contribution margin, (b) the gross profit margin.

___ 26. Fixed factory overhead should be treated as a period cost in: (a) the absorption form of income statement, (b) the contribution form of income statement, (c) both of these, (d) neither of these.

___ 27. The income statement of a manufacturing company included these amounts: selling expenses $40,000, variable factory overhead $25,000, fixed factory overhead $45,000, direct labor $60,000, general administrative expenses $35,000, direct materials used $50,000. In the contribution form of income statement, total period costs would be: (a) $180,000, (b) $120,000, (c) $75,000, (d) $145,000, (e) some other amount.

___ 28. See the preceding test item. In the absorption form of income statement, total period costs would be: (a), (b), (c), (d), (e).

___ 29. Variable factory overhead is inventoriable in: (a) the absorption form of income statement, (b) the contribution form of income statement, (c) both of these, (d) neither of these.

___ 30. The contribution form of income statement: (a) classifies costs primarily by behavior patterns, (b) facilitates cost-volume-profit analysis, (c) both of these, (d) neither of these.

Appendix

___ 31. A factory employee's wage is $12 per hour for straight time and $18 per hour for time over 40 hours per week. If the employee worked 47 hours in one week, the overtime premium would be: (a) $126, (b) $84, (c) $42, (d) none of these.

___ 32. See the preceding test item. If the employee is a product assembler who is randomly assigned to various jobs, how much should be charged to factory overhead? (a) $606, (b) $84, (c) $126, (d) none of these.

II Complete each of the following statements:

1. Expense is a cost that _____

_____ .

2. Any action or activity or part of an organization for which a separate determination of costs is desired is called _____ .

3. Minor materials that become a physical part of a manufactured product but are difficult to trace to specific product units are classified as _____

_____ .

4. Prime cost is _____

plus _____ .

5. The three main classes of inventory for a manufacturing concern are:

(a) _____

(b) _____

(c) _____

6. The traditional approach to income measurement is also known as the _____ approach.

III Classify each of these costs of Design Furniture Company as a product cost or period cost, assuming use of absorption approach:

	Product Cost	Period Cost
1. Depreciation of factory building		
2. Rental expense for retail store building		
3. Salary of company controller		
4. Paint used for finished products		
5. Public accounting fees paid		
6. Property taxes on manufacturing machinery		
7. Freight on sales to customers		
8. Supervisory salaries, factory storeroom		
9. Power for factory machines		
10. Bond interest expense		

IV For each of the transactions of Delgado Manufacturing Company shown below, indicate the effect on the company's inventories (increase, decrease, or no effect).

Transaction	Direct Materials	Work in Process	Finished Goods
1. Purchased direct materials			
2. Issued materials for use in production			
3. Incurred direct labor cost			
4. Incurred factory overhead cost			
5. Completed the finished goods			
6.(a) Sold the goods (revenues)			
6.(b) Cost of the goods sold (expenses)			
7. Incurred selling expenses			
8. Incurred general and administrative expenses			

V The income statement of Langer Products included these items (in thousands):

Sales	$960
Selling expenses (all variable)	160
Direct labor cost	210
General administrative expenses (all fixed)	90
Direct materials used	170
Fixed factory overhead costs	110

Variable factory overhead costs 50
Interest expense (fixed) 20
All inventories .... negligible

1. Assuming the absorption form of income statement is prepared, compute:

   (a) Prime cost .... $ _____

   (b) Conversion cost .... $ _____

   (c) Total product costs .... $ _____

   (d) Gross margin .... $ _____

   (e) Total period costs .... $ _____

   (f) Net income .... $ _____

2. Assuming the contribution form of income statement is used, compute:

   (a) Total variable costs .... $ _____

   (b) Total fixed costs .... $ _____

   (c) Contribution margin .... $ _____

   (d) Net income .... $ _____

VI Given for Munger Company's operations for the year ending December 31, 19X5:

Sales		$110,000
Direct material		25,000
Direct labor		22,000
Indirect manufacturing costs:		
Variable	$ 5,000	
Fixed	15,000	
Total		20,000
Selling expenses:		
Variable	$ 6,000	
Fixed	13,000	
Total		19,000
Administrative expenses:		
Variable	$ 1,000	
Fixed	11,000	
Total		12,000

1. Prepare an income statement in the absorption form (omit statement heading).

2. Prepare an income statement in the contribution form (omit heading).

CHAPTER 3 SOLUTIONS TO PRACTICE TEST QUESTIONS AND PROBLEMS

I

1 d	5 a	9 c	13 c	17 a	21 d	25 b	29 c
2 b	6 a	10 d	14 d	18 e	22 d	26 b	30 c
3 d	7 c	11 b	15 c	19 b	23 c	27 b	31 c
4 b	8 b	12 c	16 a	20 c	24 b	28 c	32 d

Computations:

10 $60,000 + 75,000 = \$135,000$ (d)
11 $43,000 + 75,000 = \$118,000$ (b)
17 $2,500 + 1,500 = \$4,000$ (a)
18 $4,200 + 3,000 = \$7,200$ (e)
22 $80 - 12 - 22 - 24 = 22$ (d)
23 $80 - 12 - 22 - (15 \div 3) - (24 \div 4) = 80 - 12 - 22 - 5 - 6 = 35$ (c)
27 $40,000 + 45,000 + 35,000 = \$120,000$ (b)
28 $40,000 + 35,000 = \$75,000$ (c)
31 $7 \times 6 = \$42$ (c)
32 $7 \times 6 = \$42$ (d)

II   1 is being deducted from revenue, 2 a cost objective, 3 factory overhead cost, 4 direct material plus direct labor, 5 direct material, work in process, and finished goods, 6 absorption approach.

III   Design Furniture Company

Product costs: 1, 4, 6, 8, 9   Period costs: 2, 3, 5, 7, 10

IV   Delgado Manufacturing Company

Transaction	Direct Materials	Work in Process	Finished Goods
1. Purchased materials	increase	no effect	no effect
2. Issued materials	decrease	increase	no effect
3. Incurred direct labor	no effect	increase	no effect
4. Incurred factory overhead	no effect	increase	no effect
5. Completed goods	no effect	decrease	increase
6.(a) Sold goods (revenues)	no effect	no effect	no effect
6.(b) Cost of goods sold	no effect	no effect	decrease
7. Selling expenses	no effect	no effect	no effect
8. Administrative expenses	no effect	no effect	no effect

V   Langer Products

1. (a) $210 + 170 = \$380$
   (b) $210 + 110 + 50 = \$370$
   (c) $210 + 170 + 110 + 50 = \$540$
   (d) $960 - 540 = \$420$
   (e) $160 + 90 + 20 = \$270$
   (f) $420 - 270 = \$150$

2. (a) $160 + 210 + 170 + 50 = \$590$
   (b) $90 + 110 + 20 = \$220$
   (c) $960 - 590 = \$370$
   (d) $370 - 220 = \$150$

VI Munger Company

1.
Absorption Income Statement

Sales		$110,000
Less manufacturing cost of goods sold:		
Direct material	$25,000	
Direct labor	$22,000	
Indirect manufacturing costs	20,000	67,000
Gross profit		$ 43,000
Less nonmanufacturing costs:		
Selling expenses	$19,000	
Administrative expenses	12,000	31,000
Operating income		$ 12,000

2.
Contribution Income Statement

Sales		$110,000
Less variable expenses:		
Direct material	$25,000	
Direct labor	$22,000	
Variable indirect manufacturing costs	5,000	
Total variable manufacturing cost of goods sold	$52,000	
Variable selling expenses	6,000	
Variable administrative expenses	1,000	
Total variable expenses		59,000
Contribution margin		$ 51,000
Less fixed expenses:		
Manufacturing	$15,000	
Selling	13,000	
Administrative	11,000	
Total fixed expenses		39,000
Operating income		$ 12,000

RELEVANT COSTS AND SPECIAL DECISIONS—PART ONE

MAIN FOCUS AND OBJECTIVES

This entire chapter is based upon one key idea—*relevant information.* This means that, when choosing among alternative courses of action, data pertinent to decisions should be confined to costs and revenues that *are expected in the future* and that *differ among the alternative actions.*

Your learning objective is to demonstrate your ability to discriminate between relevant and irrelevant information for making decisions in four practical situations:

- *Accepting or rejecting special sales orders*
- *Determining target sales prices*
- *Adding or deleting product lines*
- *Maximizing use of productive capacity*

REVIEW OF KEY IDEAS

A. Managers must choose appropriate courses of action for the future.
   1. Therefore, decisions always involve prediction.

> **Question: What is the role of historical data in the decision process?**
> **Answer: See textbook Exhibit 4-1.**

   2. As Exhibit 4-1 shows, data that are **relevant to managerial decision making** are the **predicted data** that must be compared under available alternatives.
   a. These data include only the expected future data that will differ among alternatives.

      b.   Although **historical data** are often helpful in predicting future data, **they are not relevant to the management decision itself** because they will **not differ** among alternatives.

B. The idle capacity of manufacturing facilities may allow the filling of special reduced-price sales orders that would not adversely affect the regular sales of the company.

    1. In such a case, the average overall unit costs based on data from the **absorption form** of the income statement would not serve as an appropriate basis for evaluating these orders.

> **See textbook Exhibit 4-2**

    2. The only costs that would usually be relevant to such situations are the variable costs affected by accepting the special sales orders. These costs can be more clearly identified from the **contribution form** of the income statement (also shown in Exhibit 4-2).

    3. Because fixed costs would usually not be affected by the decision, they would usually be irrelevant. However, if the decision would affect certain fixed costs, they would be relevant.

> **Question: Should special orders be accepted at selling prices below average unit costs?**
> **Answer: See textbook Exhibit 4-3.**

    4. Note in Exhibit 4-3 that there is a $100,000 advantage in accepting 100,000 units of a special order at a $13 selling price despite the fact that this is $2 less than the average absorption cost of ($12,000,000 + $3,000,000) ÷ 1,000,000 units = $15 per unit.

    5. Thus, on the basis of a relevant-cost approach, it might be quite reasonable to accept some special orders at selling prices **below** the average unit costs that include all fixed and variable costs.

    6. The important point is that such decisions should depend primarily on the revenues and costs expected to be **different** between alternatives, regardless of the form of the income statement: absorption or contribution.

    7. Although the absorption form is used for external reporting purposes, the full manufacturing cost would **not** be an appropriate base for evaluating special sales orders.

    8. You should beware of the misleading effects of **unitizing fixed costs** because this could create the false impression that these are variable costs, as demonstrated by the series of textbook examples.

C. Setting regular selling prices:

    1. Basically, three major factors influence pricing decisions: **customers, competitors,** and **costs.**

        a.   In practice, however, many managers compute their prices on the basis of certain costs, called **cost-plus pricing.**

        b.   Essentially, this method adds a "markup" to some cost figure to obtain a selling price that will generate an adequate return on investment.

    2. The textbook illustrations demonstrate that the **same target price** can be determined by four different techniques.

> **Be sure you can compute the mark-up percentages by each method. See textbook Exhibit 4-4, including the footnote.**

3. The contribution approach to pricing offers some advantages over the absorption costing approach:
    a. More detailed information is available as to variable and fixed costs.
    b. The contribution approach provides insights that help management weigh the short-term benefits of cutting prices against possible long-term disadvantages of suicidal price cutting and undermining the price structure of an industry.
4. However, the absorption costing approach has some advantages:
    a. Measures costs to recover in the long run.
    b. Measures costs that competitors might use.
    c. Simplicity: no additional data need be added to the basic accounting records.
    d. Less uncertainty in predicting demand curves.
    e. More widely acceptable for measuring costs.

D. Another management problem deals with the **deletion or addition of products or departments.**
    1. If total assets will not be affected by the decision to drop or add a product or department, some space costs and other costs will not be affected.
    2. The solution to such a case may therefore depend largely on identifying the **relevant costs** (whether fixed or variable) and measuring their effects on the **profit contribution to space and other costs,** as illustrated by the discount department store example in the textbook.
    3. In these situations, the critical cost distinction is between two types of costs that are sometimes called:
        a. **Avoidable costs,** those costs that will not continue if an ongoing operation is changed or deleted.
        b. **Unavoidable costs,** those costs that will continue, including many "common costs" of facilities and services shared by several departments or product lines.

E. Another useful illustration of the relevant-cost approach involves the question of which orders to accept when a **multiple-product plant** is being operated at capacity.

See textbook Exhibit 4-5

---

1. The criterion for maximum profits, for a given capacity, is the greatest possible contribution to profit per unit of the **limiting factor or resource.** This is the critical or scarce factor that constrains the production or sale of a given product.
2. Constraining factors are such resource measures as machine-hours, labor-hours, or cubic feet of space, and not merely the contribution-margin **ratio or percentage** considered apart from these resource measures.

PRACTICE TEST QUESTIONS AND PROBLEMS WITH SOLUTIONS

I For each of the following multiple-choice and true-false statements, select the most appropriate answer and enter its identification letter in the space provided:

____ 1. The main reason that management accountants usually try to express more decision data in quantitative terms instead of qualitative terms is because qualitative factors seldom have much weight in decision making: (a) true, (b) false.

____ 2. In the management decision process, the output from the decision model is the main input to the prediction model: (a) true, (b) false.

3. In the management decision process, the flow of historical data goes directly to the prediction model instead of the decision model: (a) true, (b) false.

4. In choosing between two alternative future actions, the decision maker should include as relevant data: (a) variable costs that are the same for the alternatives, (b) total fixed costs that are different for the alternatives, (c) both of these, (d) neither of these.

5. Costs that are relevant to decision making usually should include average fixed costs per unit that are different for the alternatives under consideration: (a) true, (b) false.

6. Past costs may sometimes be: (a) helpful in forecasting future costs, (b) relevant to decisions about the future, (c) both of these, (d) neither of these.

7. A company produces and sells 1,000 units of a product each month with total variable costs and total fixed costs of $12,000 each. Idle capacity permits the acceptance of a special sales order for 200 units each month. The average unit cost per month of producing and selling the total output, if the special order were accepted, would be: (a) $24, (b) $22, (c) $18, (d) $12.

8. See the preceding test item. The lowest unit selling price that should be accepted for the special order is: (a) $25, (b) $23, (c) $21, (d) $19.

9. When there is idle plant capacity and reduced-price special orders are received, the relevant-cost approach: (a) would evaluate the orders on the basis of average overall unit cost, (b) might indicate acceptance of orders at prices below average overall unit costs, (c) both of these, (d) neither of these.

10. Relevant data for pricing a special sales order that can be filled from idle plant capacity would include expected future unit costs of: (a) variable production costs, (b) fixed production costs, (c) both of these, (d) neither of these.

11. Each month Mon Co. manufactures 600 units of a certain product at a variable cost of $24 per unit. Total monthly fixed costs are $4,200. A special order is received for 100 units at a price of $23 per unit. Relevant to deciding to accept or reject this order is: (a) the old average fixed cost per unit: $4,200/600 = $7 per unit, (b) the new average fixed cost per unit: $4,200/700 = $6 per unit, (c) the difference between these unit costs: $7 − $6 = $1, (d) none of these figures.

12. Each month Sen Co. makes 400 units of Product C at a $40 variable cost per unit and $1,200 of total fixed costs. If a special order from a customer is accepted at a price of $42, Sen Co. will have: (a) a $1-per-unit advantage, (b) a $2-per-unit disadvantage, (c) a $2-per-unit advantage, (d) a $1-per-unit disadvantage.

13. "Unitizing fixed costs" is a helpful way of predicting the behavior of costs when fixed costs are involved: (a) true, (b) false.

14. The absorption approach makes a basic distinction between: (a) relevant and irrelevant costs, (b) past and future costs, (c) fixed and variable costs, (d) manufacturing and nonmanufacturing costs.

15. "Cost-plus pricing" adds a "markup" to cost to reach a total that is: (a) profit, (b) return on investment, (c) selling price.

16. Each month, a company has for a certain product $60,000 of total manufacturing costs (half fixed, half variable) and $20,000 of nonmanufacturing costs (half fixed and half variable). Its monthly sales are $100,000. The markup percentage on total cost to arrive at the existing (target) selling price is: (a) 10%, (b) 12.5%, (c) 20%, (d) 25%.

17. See the preceding test item. The markup percentage on total manufacturing cost to arrive at the existing (target) selling price is: (a) 67%, (b) 33%, (c) 40%, (d) 50%.

18. See item 16 above. The markup percentage on total variable cost to arrive at the

existing (target) selling price is: (a) 60%, (b) 40%, (c) 250%, (d) 150%.

___ 19. See item 16 above. The markup percentage on total variable manufacturing cost to arrive at the existing (target) selling price is: (a) 233%, (b) 30%, (c) 70%, (d) 333%.

___ 20. Although one of a company's several product lines may consistently show a net loss, its discontinuance could decrease the company's total net income: (a) true, (b) false.

___ 21. In a multiple-product plant, the criterion for maximum profits for a given capacity is the greatest: (a) contribution-margin ratio or percentage, (b) contribution to profit per unit of the limiting factor or resource.

___ 22. A company has each month 6,000 hours of plant capacity available for making two products, A and B, each with a selling price of $50 per unit. Three units of A can be made in one hour at a variable cost per unit of $35, or six units of B can be made in one hour at a variable cost per unit of $42. The number of hours that should be used each month to make A is: (a) 6,000, (b) 4,000, (c) 2,000, (d) none.

II Complete each of the following statements:

1. The costs that are relevant to managerial decision making include only the _____ _____ costs that _____ under alternative courses of action.

2. _____ costs are irrelevant to _____ but may be relevant to the prediction of future costs.

3. The absorption income statement approach subtracts _____ from _____ to arrive at gross profit.

4. The contribution income statement approach subtracts _____ from _____ to arrive at contribution margin.

5. When a multiple-product plant is being operated at capacity, the criterion for maximum profits is the largest contribution _____ _____ .

III The Two-Century Company has a monthly plant capacity of 1,500 product units. Its predicted operations for the year are:

Sales (1,000 units)	$40,000
Manufacturing costs:	
Fixed	$18,000
Variable	$15 per unit
Selling and administrative expenses:	
Fixed	$ 5,000
Variable (sales commissions)	$6 per unit

If the company accepts a special order from a customer for 300 units at a selling price of $18 each, how would the total predicted net income for the month be affected, assuming no effect on regular sales at regular prices? No sales commissions would be required by the special order, but an extra delivery cost of $770 would be required. Indicate the amount and whether it is an increase or a decrease. Ignore income taxes.

Special order sales .... $ _____

Less relevant costs:

_____ .... $ _____

_____ .... _____

Total relevant costs .... _____

Increase (or decrease) in total net income .... $ _____

IV Cost-Plus Electronics produces a pocket calculator and presents the following summary of typical operations:

	Total	Fixed	Variable
Manufacturing expenses	$ 60,000	$20,000	$40,000
Nonmanufacturing expenses	$ 40,000	$10,000	$30,000
Sales	$120,000		

Compute the markup on cost that would arrive at the target selling price, using each of the following cost bases:

1. Manufacturing cost:

2. Total cost:

3. Variable manufacturing cost:

4. Total variable cost:

V The Troika Harness Company has three product lines: Saddles, Spurs, and Blinders. The company furnished the following data for its most recent year (in millions):

	Saddles	Spurs	Blinders	Total
Sales	$45	$35	$15	$95
Avoidable fixed expenses	5	4	3	12
Unavoidable fixed expenses, allocated equally	5	5	5	15
Variable expenses	25	20	10	55
Net income (loss)	10	6	(3)	13

1. Prepare a projected operating statement using the contribution approach. Assume that the Blinders product line will be discontinued with no effects on sales of the other product lines or on the total assets used by the company.

	Saddles	Spurs	Total
Sales	$ _____	$ _____	$ _____
Less _____	_____	_____	_____
_____	_____	_____	_____
_____	_____	_____	_____
_____	_____	_____	_____
_____	$ _____	$ _____	$ _____
_____	....		_____
Net income			$ _____

2. On the basis of the statement you have prepared, would you advise the elimination of the Blinders product line?

_____ Why? _____

_____

VI Mitch Finche's Trailer Products Company has 3,600 hours of plant capacity available for manufacturing two products with the following characteristics:

	Hitches	Winches
Selling price per unit	$ 40.00	$ 30.00
Variable costs per unit	$ 30.00	$ 15.00
Units that can be manufactured in one hour (Hitches or Winches)	8 units	4 units

Compute the number of its 3,600 available production hours that this company should allocate to the manufacture of each product:

	Hitches	Winches
Selling price per unit	$ _____	$ _____
Less _____	_____	_____
_____	_____	_____
_____	_____	_____
_____	_____	_____
Contribution to profit per hour of plant capacity	$ _____	$ _____

Conclusion _____

_____

CHAPTER 4 SOLUTIONS TO PRACTICE TEST QUESTIONS AND PROBLEMS

I

1 b	4 b	7 b	10 a	13 b	16 d	19 a	22 d
2 b	5 b	8 d	11 d	14 d	17 a	20 a	
3 a	6 a	9 b	12 c	15 c	18 d	21 b	

Computations:

7 $12,000 ÷ 1,000 = $12; $12(1,000 + 200) = $14,400; ($14,400 + $12,000) ÷ (1,000 + 200) = $26,400 ÷ 1,200 = $22 (b).

8 Incremental cost per unit is $12,000 ÷ 1,000 = $12. The lowest answer given higher than this, $19 (d).

11 $24 per unit variable cost (d)

12 $42 − $40 = $2 (c)

16 (100,000 − 60,000 − 20,000) ÷ (60,000 + 20,000) = 20,000 ÷ 80,000 = 25% (d)

17 (100,000 − 60,000) ÷ 60,000 = 40,000 ÷ 60,000 = 67% (a)

18 (100,000 − 30,000 − 10,000) ÷ (30,000 + 10,000) = 60,000 ÷ 40,000 = 150% (d)

19 (100,000 − 30,000) ÷ 30,000 = 70,000 ÷ 30,000 = 233% (a)

22 No A units would be made because B has a larger contribution per available hour: 6 × (50 − 42) = $48 vs 3 × (50 − 35) = $45 (d)

II   1 expected future costs that will differ, 2 historical (or past) costs are irrelevant to the decision itself, 3 manufacturing cost of goods sold from sales to arrive at gross profit, 4 total variable expenses from sales to arrive at contribution margin, 5 to profit per unit of the limiting factor or resource.

III   Two-Century Company

Special order sales: 300 × $18		$5,400
Less relevant costs:		
Variable manufacturing costs:		
300 × $15	$4,500	
Extra delivery cost (fixed)	770	5,270
Increase in total net income		$ 130

IV   Cost-Plus Electronics

1. (120,000 − 60,000) ÷ 60,000 = 100%
2. (120,000 − 60,000 − 40,000) ÷ (60,000 + 40,000) = 20%
3. (120,000 − 40,000) ÷ 40,000 = 200%
4. (120,000 − 40,000 − 30,000) ÷ (40,000 + 30,000) = 71.4%

V   Troika Harness Company

	Saddles	Spurs	Total
1. Sales	$45	$35	$80
Less variable expenses	25	20	45
Contribution margin	$20	$15	$35
Less avoidable fixed expenses	5	4	9
Profit contribution to unavoidable costs	$15	$11	$26
Less unavoidable fixed expenses			15
Net income			$11

2. No, because the company's net income would be reduced from $13 million to $11 million without any reduction in the total assets used by the company.

VI   Mitch Finche's Trailer Products Company

	Hitches	Winches
Selling price per unit	$40.00	$30.00
Less variable costs per unit	30.00	15.00
Contribution margin per unit	$10.00	$15.00
Multiply by number of units that can be manufactured per hour	8	4
Contribution to profit and joint costs per hour of plant capacity	$80.00	$60.00

Conclusion: All 3,600 hours should be allocated to the manufacture of Hitches because they would make the larger contribution per unit of the limiting factor (hours of plant capacity).

RELEVANT COSTS AND SPECIAL DECISIONS—PART TWO

MAIN FOCUS AND OBJECTIVES

This chapter extends the application of relevant-data analysis for decision making. Remember that relevant costs and revenues consist of: *estimated future costs and revenues that differ between alternative courses of action.*

We apply this concept to four typical decisions that managers could face:

- *Make or buy certain parts or products*?
- *Process joint products beyond split-off*?
- *Scrap or remake obsolete inventory*?
- *Keep or replace old equipment*?

Be sure that you also understand how the concept of *opportunity cost* can aid decision making in these matters.

REVIEW OF KEY IDEAS

A. **Make-or-buy decisions.**
   1. These decisions may depend mainly on **qualitative factors** such as maintaining good long-term business relationships or controlling the quality of products.
   2. However, the decision may depend partly on the **quantitative measurement** of the difference in future costs between the alternatives, especially if **idle productive facilities** are involved.

> Question: Should such relevant costs be confined to variable costs?
>
> Answer: No. Relevant costs include fixed costs that can be avoided in the future (see textbook example).

3. The essence of the make-or-buy decision is how to best use facilities after considering such alternatives as:
   a. Use the facilities to make a given product.
   b. Buy the product and leave the facilities idle.
   c. Buy the product and rent out the unused facilities.
   d. Buy the product and use the facilities to make other products.
4. Make-or-buy decisions should always be related to the company's **long-term policies for using its production capacity.**

B. **Opportunity cost** is the maximum contribution or value that is given up or sacrificed by using limited resources for a given purpose.
   1. Thus the costs of choosing a particular alternative would include the benefits promised by the best of the excluded alternatives, as illustrated by the two textbook examples of the home owner and the CPA.

> **Question: Are opportunity costs ordinarily entered in the accounting records?**
> **Answer: No. They are not outlay costs because transactions have not actually occurred.**

C. When two or more products of relatively significant sales value are produced simultaneously by a single process or a series of processes, they are called **joint products.**
   1. **The split-off point** is the stage of production at which the different joint products can be individually identified:

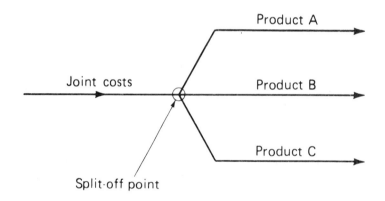

   2. **Joint costs** include all material and production costs incurred prior to the split-off point.
   3. Although the allocation of joint costs to different products is customary, this is useful only for the purposes of **costing inventory and goods sold;** joint cost allocation is **completely irrelevant** to the question of whether the individual joint products should be sold at the split-off point or processed further before being sold.
      a. The decision to process further should **not** be influenced by either the **size** of the total joint costs or the **portions** of the joint costs assigned to particular products.
      b. The only costs that are relevant to further processing decisions are the **separable costs beyond the split-off point,** which can be characterized as **differential costs.**
      c. It is profitable to process an individual product beyond the split-off point if the differential costs are **exceeded by the differential revenue** produced by such processing.

See textbook Exhibit 5-1

    d. Alternatively, you can produce the same key figures by an analysis based on the **opportunity-cost approach,** as illustrated below the exhibit.

4. The allocation of joint costs would not affect the decision to sell or process further.

See textbook Exhibit 5-2

    a. No matter how the joint costs might be allocated, the total income would not be affected.

    b. This exhibit includes both a total analysis and a **differential analysis;** thcy produce the same results and either may be used.

D. Beware of costs that are **irrelevant** to management decisions on future actions.

See textbook Exhibit 5-3

1. As pointed out earlier, **past costs** are not relevant to these decisions **per se.**

    a. The historical cost of inventory is a **past cost** that is common to all future alternatives, and thus it cannot cause **differences in expected profits** from such alternatives as scrapping the inventory or remaking it into products and selling to customers.

    b. Past costs are sometimes called **sunk costs.**

2. The **book value** of old equipment is also a past or historical cost and is therefore irrelevant to **making replacement decisions,** although it might be relevant to **developing predictions** of future cash flows that are partly dependent upon the **income tax effects** of the depreciation or sale of the equipment.

    a. However, the **disposal value** of old equipment is ordinarily relevant because it is an expected future inflow that would usually differ among alternatives.

    b. The gain or loss on disposal (the algebraic difference between book value and disposal value) is a combination of the relevant and the irrelevant and is therefore not useful for making replacement decisions.

    c. The cost of new equipment is relevant, of course, because it is an expected future cost that will differ among alternatives.

E. A serious **motivational problem** can exist in connection with the use of some decision models.

1. Consider again the equipment-replacement case in textbook Exhibit 5-3.

2. The analysis indicates a $2,500 total advantage of replacement during a four-year period.

> **Question: Why might managers nevertheless decide not to replace?**
>
> **Answer: Because they might fear a poor performance evaluation when the $1,500 loss on disposal is reported in the first year.**

3. Thus an organization might be denied a long-term benefit from replacement of the equipment.
4. The fault in logic here can result from mingling the financial impact of the **original purchase decision** with the financial impact of the **replacement decision.**
   a. Each of these two decisions should, of course, be analyzed **separately.**
   b. It would also be helpful to evaluate the manager's performance by measuring actual results against the income predictions for individual replacement decisions.
   c. However, this is often hard to do within the conventional accounting system, which is designed to report only the aggregate results of numerous decisions.

F. Expected **future costs** that will be **unaffected by decisions** are, of course, **irrelevant** to the decisions.
   1. These may include some **variable costs** as well as some fixed costs.
   2. On the other hand, expected future costs are relevant to future decisions whenever **they differ under the alternatives being considered,** and these costs may include **fixed** as well as variable costs.
   3. Thus, in relation to decisions about the future, **variable** and **fixed** should, by no means, be used as synonyms for **relevant** and **irrelevant,** respectively.

G. In arriving at decisions for replacing equipment, managers and accountants should beware of **unit costs.**
   1. **Distorted and unreliable unit costs** could be produced by irrelevant allocations of a **fixed cost** that would not be affected by the decision.
   2. Improper comparisons of **unit costs** computed at different levels of activity could lead to the wrong decision. This error can be avoided by comparing **total costs** for alternatives.

PRACTICE TEST QUESTIONS AND PROBLEMS WITH SOLUTIONS

I For each of the following multiple-choice and true-false statements, select the most appropriate answer and enter its identification letter in the space provided.

_____ 1. Some expected variable costs as well as some expected fixed costs can be irrelevant to make-or-buy decisions: (a) true, (b) false.

_____ 2. As a general rule, if a company has idle productive facilities, it should make the parts it needs instead of buying them from other manufacturers: (a) true, (b) false.

_____ 3. Costs that are relevant to make-or-buy decisions might include: (a) some historical variable costs, (b) some predicted fixed costs, (c) both of these, (d) neither of these.

_____ 4. Sly Co. need 5,000 units of a certain part. These can be purchased for $90 each, or they can be manufactured by Sly Co. by using some machinery that would otherwise be idle. The machinery has a net book value of $48,000. Amounts that are relevant to this decision include: (a) $90, (b) $48,000, (c) both the $48,000 and the $90, (d) neither the $48,000 nor the $90.

_____ 5. An opportunity cost is the lowest price available for obtaining a given product or service: (a) true, (b) false.

_____ 6. Examples of opportunity costs would include: (a) the rent expense that would have been paid by us if another alternative had been chosen, (b) the interest revenue that would have been received by us if another alternative had been chosen, (c) the salaries that would have been paid by us if another alternative had been chosen, (d) none of these.

_____ 7. Opportunity costs: (a) do not require dollar outlays, (b) are not ordinarily entered in the accounting records, (c) both of these, (d) neither of these.

___ 8. T. J. Max earns an annual salary of $30,000 as an electrician. He accepts an invitation to join an electrical contracting partnership that promises an annual profit of $38,000 to T. J. Max before the deduction of his $5,000 annual share of overhead costs. The opportunity cost of Max's decision is: (a) $5,000, (b) $8,000, (c) $3,000, (d) $35,000, (e) $33,000, (f) $30,000.

___ 9. Joint products are defined as: (a) products that are combined to make another product, (b) two or more products produced simultaneously from separate processes, (c) products that can be used in making two or more different products, (d) none of these.

___ 10. The allocation of joint costs to products is useful for: (a) determining whether to sell or to process beyond split-off, (b) costing inventory and goods sold, (c) both of these, (d) neither of these.

___ 11. Two products emerged from a joint process. Product H would have an additional market value of $14,000 after additional separable processing costs of $11,000 and allocated joint costs of $16,000. It should be: (a) sold at split-off point, (b) separately processed after split-off before being sold.

___ 12. See the preceding test item. Assume the same information except that the allocated joint costs are $11,000 and the separable costs are $16,000. The decision to sell or process further would not be different, because the total costs of Product A are unchanged: (a) true, (b) false.

___ 13. The decision to process joint products individually beyond the split-off point should depend partly upon: (a) the size of the total joint costs, (b) the portions of the joint costs allocated to particular products, (c) the method chosen for allocating joint costs, (d) none of these.

___ 14. In deciding among alternatives for using inventories, their historical cost is irrelevant if the inventories are: (a) obsolete,

(b) not obsolete, (c) both of these, (d) neither of these.

___ 15. Amounts that could be relevant to choosing among alternative uses of certain materials on hand include: (a) their salvage value, (b) their book value, (c) both of these, (d) neither of these.

___ 16. Obsolete inventory that cost $50,000 is on hand, but its scrap value is only $15,000. The inventory could be sold for $60,000 if converted into another form at an additional cost of $48,000. The **overall result** would be: (a) profit of $12,000, (b) profit of $27,000, (c) loss of $38,000, (d) loss of $23,000.

___ 17. See the preceding item. The decision should be: (a) do nothing, (b) sell the inventory for the $15,000 scrap value, (c) convert the inventory into another form and sell it for the $60,000.

___ 18. Ban Company owns a machine that has a net book value of $50,000 and a present trade-in value of $18,000 on a new machine. Each machine has an expected life of 8 years from now with terminal salvage values of $2,000 for the old machine and $12,000 for the new one. Data that are relevant to a replacement decision by Ban would include: (a) $18,000 and $50,000, (b) $50,000 and $2,000, (c) $2,000 and $12,000, (d) $12,000 and $50,000.

___ 19. Amounts that could be relevant to equipment-replacement decisions include: (a) the book value of old equipment, (b) the disposal value of old equipment, (c) both of these, (d) neither of these.

___ 20. An old machine has a scrap value of $8,000 and a net book value of $20,000. It could be used for eight more years at an annual cash operating cost of $10,000, or it could be replaced by a new machine priced at $44,000 and having an eight-year life with an annual cash operating cost of $6,000. Neither machine would have a salvage value in eight years. Ignore income taxes and the time value of money. If the company owning the old machine decides to scrap it and buy the new machine, the overall effect of this decision on the company would be: (a) an advantage of $32,000, (b) a disadvantage of $24,000, (c) a disadvantage of $11,000, (d) a disadvantage of $4,000.

___ 21. The gain or loss on disposal of old equipment: (a) can affect a manager's motivation concerning the replacement of the equipment, (b) is a helpful input to the model for making a replacement decision, (c) both of these, (d) neither of these.

___ 22. In an equipment-replacement situation, the financial impact of the replacement decision should: (a) be mingled with the financial impact of the original purchase decision, (b) not be mingled with the financial impact of the original purchase decision.

___ 23. In the comparison of fixed costs of available alternatives, it is safer to compare the costs: (a) on a unit-cost basis, (b) on a total-cost basis.

II Complete each of the following statements:

1. Irrelevant to equipment-replacement decisions is the old equipment's _____ value, but not its _____ value.

2. It is usually not profitable to process a joint product beyond the split-off point if the _____ _____ exceeds the _____ .

3. Expected future costs are not relevant to make-or-buy decisions unless _____ _____ .

4. Past or historical costs are sometimes called _____ costs.

III Wheels, Inc. incurs the following costs in making the basket for its "Little Truck" line of grocery carts:

	Total Cost for 20,000 Units	Cost per Unit
Direct materials	$ 80,000	$ 4
Direct labor	120,000	6
Variable factory overhead	40,000	2
Fixed factory overhead	120,000	6
Total costs	$360,000	$18

Another manufacturer offers to sell Wheels, Inc. the same basket for $13 per unit for 20,000 units. Determine whether Wheels should make or buy the basket, assuming the capacity now used to make the basket would become idle if it were purchased and that $50,000 of the fixed overhead could be avoided by not making the basket.

IV Lawn Supply Stores owns and operates 399 retail stores. Expected annual operating results for one of these stores are as follows:

Sales revenues	$410,000
Cost of goods sold and other direct cash operating expenses	370,000

Use the opportunity-cost concept in deciding whether to continue operations of this store or to lease the store building to a noncompeting retailer for $3,000 per month. Building ownership costs are $11,000 annually.

V Manifold Company annually produces Products T and W from a joint production process costing $195,000 per year. Each product can be sold at the split-off point or further processed before being sold:

Product	Quantity	Selling Prices per Unit At Split-Off	At Completion	Separable Processing Costs after Split-off
T	20,000	$6	$9	$52,000
W	40,000	4	5	47,000

Make an analysis to determine whether the individual products should be processed beyond the split-off point.

VI The Artstate Manufacturing Company presents the following data for a machine it owns:

Net book value $32,000
Present scrap value $12,000
Estimated remaining useful life .... 8 yrs
Predicted scrap value at end of useful life .... none
Annual cash operating costs $11,000

A new machine with the same productive capacity is available as follows:

Purchase price $43,000
Estimated useful life .... 8 yrs
Predicted scrap value at end of useful life .... none
Annual cash operating costs .... $ 6,000

1. Ignoring income taxes and the time value of money, make computations on a **total cost basis** to determine which of the two alternatives the company should select: keep the old machine or replace it with the new machine.

	Eight Years Together	
	(1) **Keep**	**(2)** **Replace**
Cash operating costs:	$ _____	$ _____
Add: _____	_____	_____
_____	_____	_____
_____	_____	_____
_____	_____	_____
_____	_____	_____
Total costs	$ _____	$ _____

Conclusion _____

2. Use the **differential approach** to reach the same conclusions determined by the total-cost approach.

CHAPTER 5 SOLUTIONS TO PRACTICE TEST QUESTIONS AND PROBLEMS

I

1 a	4 a	7 c	10 b	13 d	16 c	19 b	22 b
2 b	5 b	8 f	11 b	14 c	17 b	20 d	23 b
3 b	6 b	9 d	12 b	15 a	18 c	21 a	

Computations:

11 $14,000 − $11,000 = $3,000 incremental benefit from further processing (b). ($16,000 is irrelevant.)

12 $14,000 − $16,000 = $2,000 incremental detriment from further processing; therefore different decision (b). Allocated joint costs are irrelevant to the decisions in 11 and 12.

16 $60,000 − $50,000 − $48,000 = $38,000 overall loss (c)

17 $60,000 − $48,000 = $12,000, but this is less than the $15,000 scrap value (b)

20 ($10,000 − $6,000)(8) = $32,000, a benefit. The cost of obtaining this benefit is $44,000 − $8,000 = $36,000; $36,000 − $32,000 = $4,000 (d)

II 1 book value but not its salvage value, 2 differential (processing) cost exceeds the differential revenue, 3 they differ between alternatives, 4 sunk costs.

III Wheels, Inc.

The relevant figures to compare with the $13 purchase price are:

Direct materials	$ 80,000
Direct labor	120,000
Variable factory overhead	40,000
Avoidable fixed factory overhead	50,000
Total	$290,000 ÷ 20,000 units = $14.50

The difference in favor of buying is $14.50 − $13.00 = $1.50 for 20,000 units or $30,000 total. The same total difference could, of course, also be obtained as follows:
(20,000)($13) − $290,000 = $30,000.
Note that the unavoidable fixed overhead ($120,000 − $50,000 = $70,000) has been excluded from this analysis as being irrelevant to the decision, because it is not an expected future cost that will differ between the alternatives of making or buying the assembly.

IV Lawn Supply Stores

Sales revenues		$410,000
Less costs:		
Cost of goods sold and other direct cash expenses	$370,000	
Opportunity cost of renting: 3,000 × 12	36,000	406,000
Difference in favor of leasing		$ 4,000

(Building ownership costs are not relevant because they would be the same under each alternative.)

V   Manifold Company

Solution (a) or (b):
(a) Differential analysis:
    T $\$52,000 - \$20,000\,(\$9 - \$6) = \$52,000 - \$60,000 = \$8,000$ excess of expected benefit over related costs, decision: further process.
    W $\$47,000 - 40,000\,(\$5 - \$4) = \$47,000 - \$40,000 = (\$7,000)$ excess of expected costs over related benefit, decision: sell at split-off point.
(b) Opportunity-cost analysis:
    T $(20,000 \times \$9) - (20,000 - \$6)* - \$52,000 = \$180,000 - \$120,000* - \$52,000 = \$8,000$ as above.
    W $(40,0000 \times \$5) - (40,000 \times \$4)* - \$47,000 = \$200,000 - \$160,000* - \$47,000 = (\$7,000)$ as above.

Note that the $195,000 joint costs are irrelevant under both of these approaches.

*Opportunity cost.

VI   Artstate Manufacturing Company

1.

	Eight Years Together	
	(1) Keep	**(2) Replace**
Cash operating costs: $11,000 × 8	$ 88,000	—
$ 6,000 × 8	—	$ 48,000
Old machine total depreciation for 8 years (net book value)	32,000†	—
Old machine lump-sum write-off	—	32,000†
Disposal value of old machine	—	(12,000)
Purchase price of new machine	—	43,000
Total Costs:	$120,000	$111,000

Conclusion: Replace old machine because total costs are $9,000 lower.

2. Differential benefit: (8)($11,000 − $6,000) = $40,000
    Less cost: $43,000 − $12,000   =   31,000
    Net benefit .... $ 9,000

†Since these costs are historical costs, they are irrelevant to the decision and need not be included in such a comparison.

Chapter **6**

THE MASTER BUDGET:
THE OVERALL PLAN

MAIN FOCUS AND OBJECTIVES

The keystone of successful planning and control systems is the budget.
We focus on *the master budget*, a coordinated set of detailed operating fore-
casts for all parts of an organization.
Your objectives are to gain a useful understanding of:

- *Purposes and advantages of budgets*
- *Roles played in developing budgets*
- *Nature of the master budget framework*
- *Procedures for assembling budget data*
- *Nature and function of financial planning models*

REVIEW OF KEY IDEAS

A. Budgets are quantitative summaries of targets for operations and financial position.
   1. Activities assisted by budgets:
      a. **Financing function:** obtaining funds for investment in assets.
      b. **Operating function:** acquisition and utilization of assets.
   2. Advantages of budgets:
      a. Force management to face the task of planning, to anticipate changing conditions,
         and to formulate and implement company policies to deal with expected changes.
      b. Communicate management plans, coordinate plans, and help carry them out.
      c. Translate plans into explicit terms for evaluating actual performance in the future.
      d. An epitaph in the graveyard of bankrupt organizations:

3. **Human aspects** are more important than the mechanics of gathering and assembling data:
   a. **Participation in formulating budgets can be crucial in generating budget acceptance and management motivation to carry out plans.**

B. **The master budget**
   1. A set of forecasted financial statements sometimes called **pro-forma statements.**

> **See diagram in textbook Exhibit 6-1**

   1. The **master budget** usually summarizes a company's overall plans for one year, which can be divided into months and quarters. Such budgets can be kept continuously updated for twelve months in advance **(continuous budgets).**
   2. **Operating budgets**—such as sales, production, cost of goods sold, and expense budgets—are elements of the budgeted income statement.
   3. **Financial budgets:**
      a. Capital budget (long-range project plans)
      b. Cash budget
      c. Balance sheet
      d. Statement of changes in financial position

C. Procedures for preparing budgets:
   1. See the textbook exhibits and schedules.
   2. Conscientiously trace all steps through the model textbook example.
   3. Solve the practice test in this chapter of the study guide, especially parts III, IV, V, and VI.
   4. Note how all the budget figures are systematically tied together in VI.

D. The keystone of the entire budget structure is the **sales forecast:**

> **Question: What is the distinction between a sales forecast and a sales budget?**
> **Answer: A sales forecast is a prediction of sales under a given set of conditions. A sales budget is a result of decisions to create conditions that will generate the desired sales volume.**

1. Some factors to consider in predicting sales: past sales, competition, economic conditions, market studies.
2. Some involved personnel: line management, sales staff, economists, statisticians, research staff.

E. The master budget can serve as a **total decision model** or **financial-planning model.**

> **Question: What is a financial-planning model?**
> **Answer: Sets of mathematical statements or equations that identify the internal and external variables affecting an organization's operating and financial activities and describe their relationships.**

1. Such models aid budget preparation.
2. They can also be programmed for use on electronic data-processing equipment:
   a. To test the **sensitivity** of income and cash flows to various decisions via a **simulation**
   b. To thus quickly provide management with predicted effects of many combinations of possible choices

PRACTICE TEST QUESTIONS AND PROBLEMS WITH SOLUTIONS

I For each of the following multiple-choice and true-false statements, select the most appropriate answer and enter its identification letter in the space provided:

_____ 1. The "financing function" pertains to the acquisition and utilization of assets: (a) true, (b) false.

_____ 2. "Pro-forma statements" are prepared for comparison with budgeted financial statements at the conclusion of the budget year: (a) true, (b) false.

_____ 3. "Strategic planning": (a) sets the goals and objectives of the organization, (b) produces forecasted financial statements, (c) covers a specific period, (d) all of these.

_____ 4. The financial budget would include: (a) the budgeted balance sheet, (b) the budgeted income statement, (c) both of these, (d) neither of these.

_____ 5. The operating budget would include: (a) the cash budgets, (b) the pro-forma statement of changes in financial position, (c) both of these, (d) neither of these.

_____ 6. As a general rule, the annual budget should consist of the actual operating data for the preceding year or an average of the data for the two or three most recent years: (a) true, (b) false.

_____ 7. The main goals of budgets include: (a) limiting expenditures, (b) identifying poor performance, (c) both of these, (d) neither of these.

_____ 8. A company has a $7,200 cash balance at June 1. The budgeted cash transactions for June are receipts of $53,800 and disbursements of $67,500. If $5,000 is the company's minimum June 30 cash balance desired, what is the budgeted amount to be borrowed during June? (a) $6,500, (b) $8,700, (c) $18,700, (d) $16,500, (e) some other amount.

_____ 9. The better basis for judging actual operating results is generally considered to be: (a) past performance, (b) expected performance.

_____ 10. Budgets that are prepared for individual projects requiring an extended period of years for completion are called: (a) continuous budgets, (b) operating budgets, (c) master budgets, (d) capital budgets.

____ 11. In the preparation of a budget for merchandise purchases during a given period, consideration should normally be given to: (a) the desired ending inventory for the period, (b) the beginning inventory for the period, (c) both of these, (d) neither of these.

____ 12. A merchandising company has $64,000 of accounts receivable at April 30. In May it expects to collect 75% of these receivables and 30% of the May sales on account. Its budgeted sales on account for May are $70,000. The budgeted accounts receivable at May 31 would be: (a) $69,000, (b) $65,000, (c) $37,000, (d) $97,000, (e) some other amount.

____ 13. The pattern of collections of accounts receivable for a company is 20% in month of sale, 50% in the following month, and 30% in the month after that. Sales on account were $80,000 for January and $60,000 for February. Budgeted sales for March are $70,000. Compute the budgeted cash collections in March: (a) $65,000, (b) $70,000, (c) $68,000, (d) $72,000, (e) some other amount.

____ 14. See the preceding test item and assume all the same data plus budgeted sales of $100,000 for April. Compute the budgeted cash collections in April: (a) $56,000, (b) $73,000, (c) $66,000, (d) $83,000, (e) some other amount.

____ 15. A merchandising company forecasts

$150,000 of sales for September. Its gross profit rate is 40% of sales, and its August 31 merchandise inventory is $112,000. Compute the budgeted purchases for September if the company wishes to budget an inventory of $122,000 for the end of September: (a) $70,000, (b) $50,000, (c) $80,000, (d) $100,000, (e) some other amount.

____ 16. See the preceding item and assume that all data are the same except that the gross profit rate is 60%. The budgeted purchases for September would be: (a) $70,000, (b) $50,000, (c) $80,000, (d) $100,000, (e) some other amount.

II Complete each of the following statements:

1. A budget that is regularly updated to show a one-year forecast by adding a month or quarter in the future as the month or quarter just ended is dropped is called a _____ budget.

2. In general, it is usually best to start with a forecast of _____ in constructing a master budget.

3. Budgeted merchandise purchases for a given period may be computed by adding _____ _____ to budgeted cost of goods sold and subtracting the _____ _____ from this total.

III Given for RACO Co. (in thousands):

	April Actual	May Actual	June Budgeted	July Budgeted
Cash sales	$ 80	$ 50	$ 70	$ 90
Sales on account	320	200	300	280

Compute the budgeted cash receipts for June and July, assuming credit sales are collected as follows: 15% in month of sale, 60% in the following month, and 25% in the month after that:

June: _____

July: _____

IV Given for Worldly Goods, Inc.

	April	July
Beginning merchandise inventory	$ 18,400	$ 31,900
Expected sales	160,000	180,000
Desired ending merchandise inventory	21,000	30,000
Expected gross profit rate on sales	30%	40%
Find the budgeted purchases for each month	$ _____	$ _____

Exp. CGS
+ EI
– BI
Exp PuR

V Given for Floor Veneer Products

	September	November
Beginning cash balance	$16,100	$15,600
Expected cash receipts	62,900	71,600
Expected cash disbursements	45,200	77,300
Minimum ending cash balance desired	12,000	14,000

Find the estimated amount (1. or 2.) for each month:

1. Necessary to borrow	$ _____	$ _____
2. Available for repayment of loans and interest	$ _____	$ _____

VI The Four-Sight Lens Company presented the following balance sheet at March 31, 19X4, the beginning of a budget period:

Current assets:

Cash	$ 9,500	
Accounts receivable	33,300	
Merchandise inventory	66,600	
Total current assets		$109,400
Plant and equipment	$45,000	
Less accumulated depreciation	18,000	
Net plant and equipment		27,000
Total assets		$136,400

Current liabilities:

Accounts payable	$27,700	
Accrued taxes payable	4,200	
Total current liabilities		$ 31,900
Owners' equity		104,500
Total liabilities and owners' equity		$136,400

The company's budgeted operations for the month of April 19X4 are shown below:

Cash receipts:

From cash sales	$ 14,800
From collections of accounts receivable	20,100
Total	$ 34,900

Cash disbursements:

For operating expenses	$ 14,500
For payments on accounts payable	17,000
Total	$ 31,500

Other transactions:

Sales of merchandise on account	$ 25,000
Purchases of merchandise (all on account)	18,500
Depreciation of plant and equipment	300
Additional accrued taxes	1,200
Cost of goods sold	22,300

Using the forms provided below, prepare the following:

1. The detailed budget schedules, (a) through (h), for April 19X4.
2. The budgeted income statement for April 19X4.
3. The budgeted balance sheet at April 30, 19X4.

1. Detailed budget schedules:

(a) Sales for April 19X4:

Cash sales	$ _____
Sales on account	_____
Total budgeted sales for April 19X4:	$ _____

(b) Cash balance at April 30, 19X4:

	Cash	$ 9,500
	Cash Sales	14,800
	AR	20,100
	– Dis	31,500
		$ 12,900

(c) Accounts receivable at April 30, 19X4:

	Bal	$ 33,300
	Rec	– 20,100
	AC	+ 25,000
		$ 38,200

(d) Merchandise inventory at April 30, 19X4:

	BI	$ 66,600
	Pur	+ 18,500
	CGS	– 22,300
		$ 62,800

(e) Accumulated depreciation at April 30, 19X4:

		$ 18,000
	+	300
		$ 18,300

(f) Accounts payable at April 30, 19X4:

	Beg	$ 27,700
	pd –	17,000
	bought +	18,500
		$ 29,200

(g) Accrued taxes payable at April 30, 19X4:

	Beg	$ 4200
	N.u	1200
		$ 5400

(h) Owners' equity at April 30, 19X4:

	B	$ 104,500
A – L = OE		1,500
		$ 106,000

2. Budgeted income statement:

Sales (Schedule a) .... $ _____39,800_____

Less _____ _____22,300_____

Gross _____ _____17,500_____

Less expenses:

_____	Op	$ _____14,500_____
_____	Dep	_____300_____
_____	Tax	_____1,200_____

Total expenses .... _____16,000_____

Net income .... $ _____1500_____

3. Budgeted balance sheet:

Current assets:

Cash (Schedule b) .... $ _____12,900_____

_____AR_____ (Schedule _C_) _____38,200_____

_____INV_____ (Schedule _D_) _____62,800_____

Total current assets .... $ _____113,900_____

Plant and equipment .... $ _____45,000_____

Less accumulated depreciation (Schedule e) .... _____18,300_____

Net plant and equipment .... _____26,700_____

Total assets .... $ _____87200_____

Current liabilities:

_____AP_____ (Schedule _F_) $ _____29,200_____

_____Taxes Pay_____ (Schedule _g_) _____5400_____

Total current liabilities .... $ _____34600_____

Owner's equity (Schedule h) .... _____106,000_____

Total liabilities and owners' equity .... $ _____140,600_____

CHAPTER 6 SOLUTIONS TO PRACTICE QUESTIONS AND PROBLEMS

I   1 b   3 a   5 d   7 d   9 b   11 c   13 c   15 d

     2 b   4 a   6 b   8 e   10 d   12 b   14 b   16 a

Computations

8   $67,500 + 5,000 - 7,200 - 53,800 = \$11,500$ (e)

12   $64,000 - 75\%(64,000) + 70,000 - 30\%(70,000) = 16,000 + 49,000 = \$65,000$ (b)

13   $30\%(80,000) + 50\%(60,000) + 20\%(70,000) = 24,000 + 30,000 + 14,000 = \$68,000$ (c)

14   $30\%(60,000) + 50\%(70,000) + 20\%(100,000) = 18,000 + 35,000 + 20,000 = \$73,000$ (b)

15   $150,000 - 40\%(150,000) = 90,000; 90,000 + 122,000 - 112,000 = \$100,000$ (d)

16   $150,000 - 60\%(150,000) = 60,000; 60,000 + 122,000 - 112,000 = \$70,000$ (a)

II   1 continuous, 2 sales, 3 the desired or planned ending inventory, beginning inventory.

III   RACO Co.

June: $70 + 25\%(320) + 60\%(200) + 15\%(300) = 70 + 80 + 120 + 45 = \$315$

July: $90 + 25\%(200) + 60\%(300) + 15\%(280) = 90 + 50 + 180 + 42 = \$362$

IV   Worldly Goods, Inc.

	April	July
Expected cost of goods sold: 70%(160,000)	$112,000	
60%(180,000)		$108,000
Add desired ending inventory	21,000	30,000
Total needs	$133,000	$138,000
Less beginning inventory	18,400	31,900
Budgeted merchandise purchases	$114,600	$106,100

V   Floor Veneer Products

	September	November
Beginning cash balance	$16,100	$15,600
Add expected cash receipts	62,900	71,600
Total available before current financing (a)	$79,000	$87,200
Expected cash disbursements	$45,200	$77,300
Add minimum ending cash balance desired	12,000	14,000
Total cash needed (b)	$57,200	$91,300
1. Necessary to borrow: (b) − (a)		$ 4,100
2. Available for repayment of loans and interest:		
(a) − (b)	$21,800	

VI   Four-Sight Lens Company

   1. Budget schedules:

     (a) Sales for April 19X4:

Cash sales	$ 14,800
Sales on account	25,000
Total budgeted sales for April 19X4	$ 39,800

(b) Cash balance at April 30, 19X4:

Cash balance at March 31, 19X4	$ 9,500
Add total budgeted cash receipts for April	34,900
Total	$ 44,400
Less total budgeted cash disbursements for April	31,500
Budgeted cash balance at April 30, 19X4	$ 12,900

(c) Accounts receivable at April 30, 19X4:

Accounts receivable at March 31, 19X4	$ 33,300
Add budgeted sales on account for April	25,000
Total	$ 58,300
Less budgeted cash collections on account for April	20,100
Budgeted accounts receivable at April 30, 19X4	$ 38,200

(d) Merchandise inventory at April 30, 19X4:

Merchandise inventory at March 31, 19X4	$ 66,600
Add budgeted purchases for April	18,500
Total	$ 85,100
Less budgeted cost of goods sold for April	22,300
Budgeted merchandise inventory at April 30, 19X4	$ 62,800

(e) Accumulated depreciation at April 30, 19X4:

Accumulated depreciation at March 31, 19X4	$ 18,000
Add budgeted depreciation for April	300
Budgeted accumulated depreciation at April 30, 19X4	$ 18,300

(f) Accounts payable at April 30, 19X4:

Accounts payable at March 31, 19X4	$ 27,700
Add budgeted merchandise purchases on account for April	18,500
Total	$ 46,200
Less budgeted payments on accounts payable for April	17,000
Budgeted accounts payable at April 30, 19X4	$ 29,200

(g) Accrued taxes payable at April 30, 19X4:

Accrued taxes payable at March 31, 19X4	$ 4,200
Add additional accrued taxes budgeted for April	1,200
Budgeted accrued taxes payable at April 30, 19X4	$ 5,400

(h) Owners' equity at April 30, 19X4:

Owners' equity at March 31, 19X4	$104,500
Add budgeted net income for April (from budgeted income statement for April)	1,500
Budgeted owners' equity at April 30, 19X4	$106,000

2. Budgeted income statement:

Sales (Schedule a)		$ 39,800
Less cost of goods sold		22,300
Gross margin on sales		$ 17,500
Less expenses:		
Operating expenses	$14,500	
Depreciation	300	
Taxes	1,200	
Total expenses		16,000
Net income		$ 1,500

3. Budgeted balance sheet:

Current assets:

Cash (Schedule b)	$12,900	
Accounts receivable (Schedule c)	38,200	
Merchandise inventory (Schedule d)	62,800	
Total current assets		$113,900
Plant and equipment	$45,000	
Less accumulated depreciation (Schedule e)	18,300	
Net plant and equipment		26,700
Total assets		$140,600

Current liabilities:

Accounts payable (Schedule f)	$29,200	
Accrued taxes payable (Schedule g)	5,400	
Total current liabilities		$ 34,600
Owners' equity (Schedule h)		106,000
Total liabilities and owners' equity		$140,600

Chapter 7

FLEXIBLE BUDGETS AND STANDARDS FOR CONTROL

MAIN FOCUS AND OBJECTIVES

Part One of the chapter refines the budget concept by distinguishing between *static budgets* and *flexible budgets*. The key textbook Exhibit 7-4 is a useful framework for measuring operating results against these budgets. Be sure that you thoroughly grasp the meaning of the three basic types of variances:

- *Flexible-budget variances*
- *Sales-volume variances*
- *Master (static)-budget variances*

Part Two introduces *standard costs* and explains how flexible-budget cost variances are subdivided for management control purposes into *price variances* and *efficiency variances*. Be able to compute these and apply them to a performance analysis.

REVIEW OF KEY IDEAS

Part One

A. **Flexible Budget:**
  1. Prepared for a **range** of expected activity
  2. For example, see textbook Exhibit 7-2
  3. Contrast with a **static budget** (the **master budget**), which is tied to a **single** activity level

B. **Budget Formula:** used to prepare a flexible budget.
  1. For **strictly variable costs,** this formula is the **cost rate per unit of product or activity,** thus permitting each cost in the budget to be easily adjusted later to serve as a comparison basis for the particular activity level actually attained, as shown in the upper part of Exhibit 7-2.

2. For **fixed costs,** the budget formula is simply the total predetermined amounts per month or other budget period, illustrated in the lower part of Exhibit 7-2.
3. The relationship between these two formulas is portrayed by the graph of total costs in Exhibit 7-3.

C. **Budget Variances:**
1. **Sales-volume variance** is the difference between the master (static)-budget amount and the flexible-budget amount.
2. **Flexible-budget variance** is the difference between the flexible-budget amount and the actual result.
   a. See also Exhibit 7-5.
   b. We learn in Part Two of the chapter how these variances are subdivided into **price** and **efficiency variances.**
3. **Master (static)-budget variance** is the difference between the actual result and the master (static)-budget amount.

> **Question: Is this the sum of 1 and 2 above?**
> **Answer: Yes. See textbook Exhibit 7-4.**

Part Two

D. **Standard Costs:**
1. **Definition:** carefully predetermined unit costs used as yardsticks for evaluating actual performance.
2. **Perfection standards,** also often called **ideal standards,** are expressions of the absolute minimum unit costs possible under the best conceivable conditions, using current specifications and facilities (not widely used).
3. **Currently attainable standards** represent costs that should be incurred under very efficient operations.
   a. These standards do make allowances for normal shrinkage, spoilage, lost time, and machinery breakdowns.
   b. Such standards may be used simultaneously for budgeting, inventory valuation, and performance measurement.
   c. Currently attainable standards usually have a **desirable motivational effect** on employees because, although difficult to reach, they are accepted as reasonable goals.
   d. If standards are currently attainable, as we assume in this book, they are conceptually the same as budgets except that we will view **standards** in terms of **unit costs** and **budgets** in terms of **total costs.**

E. **Flexible-Budget Cost Variances:**
1. **Price variances** for direct materials, direct labor, and variable overhead items like supplies are computed as:

(Actual inputs purchased)
×
(Difference between actual and standard prices)

2. **Efficiency variances** are:

(Standard prices)
×
(Difference between actual and standard inputs)

3. Synonyms:
   a. Price variances are often called **rate variances** when referring to labor.
   b. Efficiency variances are also called **quantity variances** and **usage variances.**
4. Exhibit 7-8 shows an analysis of factory overhead variance:
   a. Variable overhead flexible-budget variance can be subdivided into spending variance and efficiency variance.
   b. Fixed overhead flexible budget variance is not subdivided (more in Chapter 15).

F. Variance Control:
1. Direct-material variances:
   a. The responsibility for material price variances usually lies with the **purchasing executive** of a manufacturing company or with the **merchandise manager** of a nonmanufacturing company.
   b. It is usually more desirable to determine such price variances either at the time the purchase order is prepared or when the purchase invoice is received, not later when the materials are used.
   c. The responsibility for material efficiency variances usually rests with the **production executive** of a manufacturing company or the **store manager** of a retail establishment.
2. Direct-labor variances:
   a. Generally, because of union contracts, labor prices can be predicted much more accurately than can material prices.
   b. Moreover, labor price and efficiency variances occur together because the acquisition and use of labor take place **simultaneously.**
   c. Therefore, labor price variances are usually the responsibility of the same manager who is in charge of labor usage.
3. Variance analysis does **not** provide any answers; it only raises questions, provides clues, and directs management attention to certain problems. Thus it is subject to some important limitations. Dividing flexible-budget cost variances into price and efficiency elements is only a **first step** in analysis.

PRACTICE TEST QUESTIONS AND PROBLEMS WITH SOLUTIONS

I For each of the following multiple-choice and true-false statements, select the most appropriate answer and enter its identification letter in the space provided:

___ 1. The master-budget variance is the difference between: (a) flexible budget and master budget, (b) actual results and flexible budget, (c) master budget and actual results, (d) none of these.

___ 2. The flexible-budget variance is the difference between: (a) flexible budget and actual results, (b) master budget and flexible budget, (c) actual results and master budget, (d) none of these.

___ 3. Sales-volume variance plus flexible-budget variance equals master-budget variance: (a) true, (b) false.

___ 4. The sales-volume variance is the difference between the flexible budget and the master budget: (a) true, (b) false.

___ 5. The main flexible-budget variances are: (a) price and rate, (b) quantity and efficiency, (c) usage and quantity, (d) price and usage.

_____ 6. A summary of performance showed three amounts for variable costs: actual $180,000, static budget $185,000, and flexible budget $170,000. The sales-volume variance is: (a) $15,000 favorable, (b) $5,000 favorable, (c) $10,000 unfavorable, (d) $5,000 unfavorable.

_____ 7. See the preceding test item. The flexible-budget variance is: (a), (b), (c), (d).

_____ 8. A summary of performance showed three figures for contribution margin: flexible budget $90,000, master budget $110,000, and actual results $92,000. The sales-volume variance is: (a) $2,000 favorable, (b) $2,000 unfavorable, (c) $18,000 favorable, (d) $20,000 unfavorable.

_____ 9. See the preceding test item. The flexible-budget variance is: (a), (b), (c), (d).

_____ 10. The most widely used type of standard costs is: (a) the perfection standard, (b) a currently attainable standard.

_____ 11. There is no conceptual difference between a budget amount and a standard amount if standards are: (a) ideal standards, (b) perfection standards, (c) currently attainable standards, (d) flexible standards.

_____ 12. Standards that tend to have a more positive effect on employee motivation are: (a) perfection standards, (b) currently attainable standards.

_____ 13. An unfavorable material efficiency variance could be calculated by multiplying the quantity of excess materials used by: (a) actual material unit prices, (b) standard material unit prices.

_____ 14. The labor efficiency variance is found by multiplying a certain figure by the difference between the actual labor hours and the standard hours allowed for the actual number of product units produced. This figure is: (a) the actual labor cost per hour, (b) the standard labor cost per hour.

_____ 15. Data for a certain operation included a $9 standard wage rate per hour, a $10 actual wage rate per hour, 800 actual labor-hours used, 250 product units produced, and 3 standard labor-hours allowed per product unit. The labor price variance is: (a) $800 unfavorable, (b) $800 favorable, (c) $750 unfavorable, (d) $500 unfavorable, (e) $500 favorable, (f) $450 unfavorable.

_____ 16. See the preceding test item. The labor efficiency variance is: (a), (b), (c), (d), (e), (f).

_____ 17. Data for a certain operation included a $20 standard material cost per pound, a $19 actual material cost per pound, 110 actual material pounds used, 30 product units produced, and 4 standard material pounds allowed per product unit. The material price variance is: (a) $190 favorable, (b) $200 unfavorable, (c) $200 favorable, (d) $110 favorable, (e) $110 unfavorable, (f) $120 favorable.

_____ 18. See the preceding test item. The material efficiency variance is: (a), (b), (c), (d), (e), (f).

_____ 19. Labor price variances are usually the responsibility of the same manager who is in charge of labor usage: (a) true, (b) false.

_____ 20. Generally, the cost variances that are more subject to immediate management control are: (a) price variances, (b) efficiency variances.

_____ 21. For most effective control, material price variances should be measured at the time materials are: (a) purchased, (b) used, (c) sold to customers.

_____ 22. In practice, the joint price-efficiency variance is usually included as part of the: (a) price variance, (b) efficiency variance.

II Complete each of the following statements:

1. Standard costs that make no allowance for lost time, spoilage, shrinkage, or machinery break-

downs are called _____ standards.

2. Standard costs that may be used simultaneously for budgeting, inventory valuation, and performance measurement are called _____

_____ standards.

3. When currently attainable standards are used, we view _____ in terms of unit

costs and _____ in terms of total costs.

4. Material price variances are usually the responsibility of the _____

_____

_____ .

5. The material price variance is computed as the difference between actual and standard unit prices multiplied by _____

_____ .

III Immerman, Inc. presents the following data pertaining to its total manufacturing costs for a given month:

Static budget for production of 8,000 units $520,000
Actual costs of producing 7,000 units 471,000
Flexible-budget formula: $200,000 plus $40 per unit

Compute the following:

1. Flexible budget for actual output achieved .... $ _____

2. Sales-volume variance .... $ _____

3. Flexible-budget variance .... $ _____

4. Master-budget variance .... $ _____

IV Primordial Co., which uses standard costs and a flexible budget, provides the following data for its operations during last month:

Finished units produced	500 units
Standard labor-hours allowed per product unit	5 hours
Standard wage rate per hour	$10
Actual wage rate per hour	$11
Total direct-labor-hours actually used	2,600 hours

Show calculation of direct-labor costs and variances in the analysis framework given below. Ignore payroll taxes, all other payroll deductions, and fringe labor costs. Use F for favorable variances and U for unfavorable variances.

Cost Incurred: Actual Inputs X Actual Prices	Actual Inputs X Standard Prices	Flexible Budget: Standard Prices X Standard Inputs Allowed
_____	_____	_____
_____	_____	_____
_____	_____	_____
_____	_____	_____

↑ **Labor Price Variance** ↑ **Labor Efficiency Variance** ↑

↑ **Total Flexible-Budget Variance for Direct Labor** ↑

V Superb Corporation, which uses standard costs and a flexible budget, provides the following data for its operations during the first week in April:

Finished product units produced	3,000 units
Direct material:	
Purchases	9,000 lb
Standard price per pound	$8
Actual price per pound	$7
Pounds used in production	7,000 lb
Standard quantity allowed per product unit	2 lb

Suppose the company is organized so that the purchasing manager bears the primary responsibility for the acquisition prices of materials, and the production manager bears the primary responsibility for the efficient use of materials but no responsibility for unit prices, as in Part 2 of Summary Problem Two of the textbook.

Show computations of direct material costs and variances in the analysis framework given below. Use F for favorable variances and U for unfavorable variances.

Control Point	Cost Incurred: Actual Quantity X Actual Price	Actual Quantity X Standard Price	Flexible Budget: Standard Price X Standard Quantity Allowed
Purchasing	_____	_____	
Department	_____	_____	

↑ **Material Price Variance** ↑

_____

Production		_____	_____
Department		_____	_____

↑ **Material Efficiency Variance** ↑

_____

CHAPTER 7 SOLUTIONS TO PRACTICE TEST QUESTIONS AND PROBLEMS

I

1 c	5 d	9 a	13 b	17 d	21 a
2 a	6 a	10 b	14 b	18 c	22 a
3 a	7 c	11 c	15 a	19 a	
4 a	8 d	12 b	16 f	20 b	

Computations:

6 $185,000 - 170,000 = \$15,000$ favorable (a)

7 $180,000 - 170,000 = \$10,000$ unfavorable (c)

8 $110,000 - 90,000 = \$20,000$ unfavorable (d)

9 $92,000 - 90,000 = \$2,000$ favorable (a)

15 $(800 \times \$10) - (800 \times \$9) = \$8,000 - \$7,200 = \$800$
unfavorable (a); or $800 \times (\$10 - \$9) = \$800$

16 $(250 \times 3 \times \$9) - (800 \times \$9) = \$6,750 - \$7,200 = \$450$
unfavorable (f); or $800 - (3 \times 250) = 50; 50 \times \$9 = \$450$

17 $(110 \times \$19) - (110 \times \$20) = \$2,090 - \$2,200 = \$110$
favorable (d); or $(\$20 - \$19)(110) = \$110$

18 $(30 \times 4 \times \$20) - (110 \times \$20) = \$2,400 - \$2,200 = \$200$
favorable (c); or $110 - (30 \times 4) = 10; 10 \times \$20 = \$200$

II   1 perfection (or ideal) standards, 2 currently attainable standards, 3 standards in terms of unit costs and budgets in terms of total costs, 4 purchasing executive of a manufacturing company or the merchandise manager of a nonmanufacturing company, 5 the actual quantity purchased.

III   Immerman, Inc.

1. $200,000 + 40(7,000) = \$480,000$

2. $520,000 - 480,000 = \$40,000$ F

3. $480,000 - 471,000 = \$9,000$ F

4. $520,000 - 471,000 = \$49,000$ F

IV   Primordial Co.

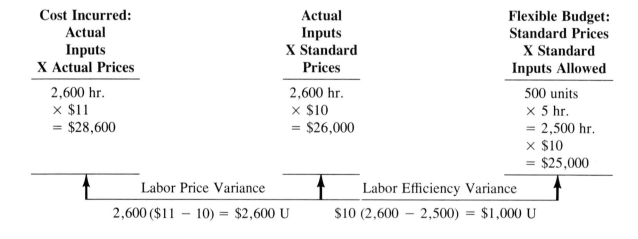

Cost Incurred: Actual Inputs X Actual Prices		Actual Inputs X Standard Prices		Flexible Budget: Standard Prices X Standard Inputs Allowed
2,600 hr. × \$11 = \$28,600		2,600 hr. × \$10 = \$26,000		500 units × 5 hr. = 2,500 hr. × \$10 = \$25,000

Labor Price Variance

Labor Efficiency Variance

$2,600 (\$11 - 10) = \$2,600$ U $\$10 (2,600 - 2,500) = \$1,000$ U

Total Flexible-Budget Variance for Direct Labor

$\$28,600 - \$25,000 = \$3,600$ U or $\$2,600 + \$1,000 = \$3,600$ U

V   Superb Corporation

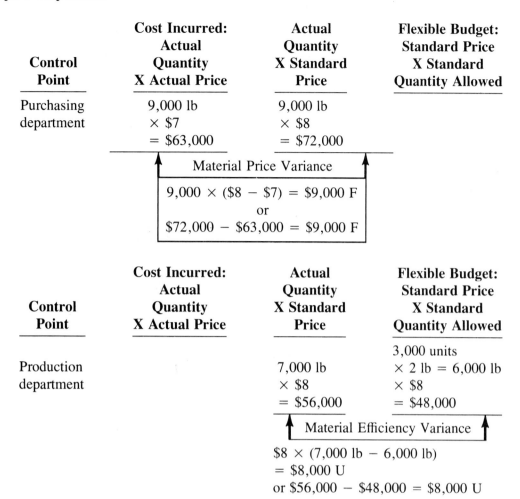

Control Point	Cost Incurred: Actual Quantity X Actual Price	Actual Quantity X Standard Price	Flexible Budget: Standard Price X Standard Quantity Allowed
Purchasing department	9,000 lb × $7 = $63,000	9,000 lb × $8 = $72,000	

Material Price Variance

9,000 × ($8 − $7) = $9,000 F
or
$72,000 − $63,000 = $9,000 F

Control Point	Cost Incurred: Actual Quantity X Actual Price	Actual Quantity X Standard Price	Flexible Budget: Standard Price X Standard Quantity Allowed
Production department		7,000 lb × $8 = $56,000	3,000 units × 2 lb = 6,000 lb × $8 = $48,000

Material Efficiency Variance

$8 × (7,000 lb − 6,000 lb)
= $8,000 U
or $56,000 − $48,000 = $8,000 U

Chapter **8**

VARIATIONS OF COST BEHAVIOR
PATTERNS

MAIN FOCUS AND OBJECTIVES

Previously, we identified two mutually exclusive patterns of cost behavior—strictly fixed and strictly variable. Now we introduce some useful subclassifications for management planning and control:

- *Committed and discretionary fixed costs*
- *Engineered and discretionary variable costs*

We learn how costs are influenced by *management discretion* in conjunction with activity volume. The chapter focuses mainly on methods of predicting costs for budget purposes. Important techniques include:

- *Work measurement approach*
- *Negotiated static budgets*
- *Methods to determine cost functions*

REVIEW OF KEY IDEAS

A. Fixed costs, also called **capacity costs,** originate from outlays for assets, people, and programs. These outlays measure a company's cost of providing a particular capacity for such activities as production, sales, administration, and research.
  1. **Committed fixed costs** are incurred because of a company's basic organization and the ownership of such long-term assets as land, buildings, machinery, and equipment.
    a. Examples are certain administrative salaries, insurance, property taxes, rent, depreciation, and long-term lease payments.
    b. Committed fixed costs, the least responsive of fixed costs to short-term decisions, cannot be decreased without jeopardizing a company's ability to meet its long-range goals.
    c. Thus capital expenditures, which lay the foundation for many fixed costs, must be planned very carefully.

      d. Once capital expenditures are made, the basic control approach is to increase the **current utilization** of the facilities.

2. Discretionary fixed costs, also called **managed or programmed costs,** arise from periodic budget appropriation decisions to implement top management policies.

      a. Examples include the costs of advertising, sales promotion, employee training programs, and research and development.

      b. Discretionary fixed costs usually do not depend directly on the volume of activity but are determined in advance by management for the budget period.

3.

> **Question: How do discretionary fixed costs contrast to: (a) committed fixed costs and (b) typical variable costs?**
> **Answers: See below.**

      a. In contrast to committed fixed costs, discretionary fixed costs could be drastically reduced if bad times are anticipated for a given period.

      b. In contrast to typical variable costs, discretionary fixed costs usually cannot be evaluated systematically and reliably in terms of their benefits to the organization ("input-output analysis").

B. Variable costs, in general, are expected to fluctuate, in total, directly in proportion to sales volume, production volume, or some other measure of activity.

    1. They usually have an explicit **engineered** or **physical relationship** to volume.

    2. Such variable costs may have a **strict linear variability,** for example, the cost of materials and parts used to produce certain kinds of finished products.

    3. However, not to be confused with "engineered" variable costs are a few other variable costs, such as advertising and research, that may fluctuate with sales merely because management has allocated in advance certain proportions of dollar sales for these purposes. These are called **discretionary variable costs.**

C. Work measurement is a formal analysis of a task, its size, the methods used in its performance, and its efficiency. This can be viewed as an **engineered variable-cost approach** to controlling costs.

    1. The objective of work measurement is to determine the workload in an operation and the number of employees necessary to perform that workload efficiently.

    2. By using such techniques as time-and-motion study, one can set **perfection standards** that can indicate in advance the number of **control-factor units** needed for a given quantity of some specified work, for example, the number of operations per hour for a certain clerical activity.

      a. These standards aid in the analysis of the efficiency and effectiveness with which resources are being used to do the work.

      b. This is done by using the standard to determine the flexible budget for a particular expense and thus to compute the **budget variance:** actual cost minus the flexible-budget amount.

> **See the $1,080 unfavorable budget variance in the textbook example of payroll-clerk labor.**

    3. However, most organizations do not use work-measurement techniques for controlling nonmanufacturing costs.

      a. Instead, they usually treat such costs in their budgets as **discretionary fixed costs.**

    b. The actual expenditures are then periodically examined to see that the available resources are being properly utilized.

D. Discretionary fixed costs are usually controlled by **negotiated static budgets.**
    1. The **incremental approach** is traditional.
    2. However, **zero-base budgeting (ZBB)** is sometimes used.
        a. This means that costs (and revenues in some cases) should be justified as though they were being incurred **for the first time.**

E. In determining cost behavior patterns **(cost functions),** cost accountants have developed feasible methods by making trade-offs between accuracy and simplicity.
    1. As a result, two common assumptions are usually made concerning cost behavior:
        a. **Only one independent variable** (for example, labor-hours or machine-hours) is needed for an adequate explanation of cost behavior.
        b. **Linear approximations** to cost functions are often satisfactory reflections of the actual behavior.
    2. The general formula for a linear cost function is:

$$y = a + bx.$$

        a. The variable to be predicted is **y,** the **dependent variable;** for example, power cost.
        b. The other variable is **x,** the **independent variable;** for example, machine-hours.
        c. The **intercept** is **a,** the value of **y** when **x** is zero.
        d. The **slope** of the line is **b,** the amount of increase in **y** for each unit of increase in **x.**
        e. The **parameters** are **a** (a **constant**) and **b** (a **coefficient**).
    3. The major types of cost functions in addition to fixed and variable costs, which have already been defined, are:
        a. **Mixed** or **semivariable costs,** a combination of variable and fixed costs.
        b. **Step-function costs,** a nonlinear cost with abrupt breaks in the behavior pattern of total cost as activity volume shifts from one range to another.
    4. Two principal criteria are used for accepting and using a particular cost function:
        a. **Economic plausibility.** The relationship must seem reasonable, the most convincing evidence usually being personal observation.
        b. **Goodness of fit.** These are technical tests such as scatter diagrams and regression analysis.
        c. These two criteria are interrelated and must be used jointly.
    5. Six methods of approximating cost functions are described briefly in the textbook: industrial engineering, detailed ledger account analysis, high-low points, visual fit, simple regression, and multiple regression.

F. Mixed costs are used in the textbook to illustrate how to approximate a cost function.
    1. Examples of mixed costs include repairs, power, and the rental of a truck at a fixed monthly rate plus a mileage rate (see textbook Exhibit 8-1).
    2. Ideally, the fixed and variable-cost elements should be budgeted separately and included in **different** ledger accounts. In practice, however, mixed costs are generally **combined** in single ledger accounts.
    3. Nevertheless, mixed costs can be budgeted by using a separate formula for each cost element.
    4. The **high-low method** can sometimes be useful in separating fixed costs, but it must be used cautiously, especially when applied to a wide range of volume.

a. To be sure you can use this simple method, follow the textbook example very closely.

See textbook Exhibit 8-2

---

5. The **visual-fit method** uses all data points instead of the two used by the high-low method.
   a. A **scatter-diagram** helps to determine whether the relationship is approximately linear (see textbook Exhibit 8-3).
6. The **least-squares method** is a mathematical approach that uses all available data in a more objective way than the visual-fit method.
   a. This method also provides statistics to show how well the regression line fits the data (see textbook Exhibit 8-4).
   b. More details are covered in the chapter appendix.

PRACTICE TEST QUESTIONS AND PROBLEMS WITH SOLUTIONS

I For each of the following multiple-choice and true-false statements, select the most appropriate answer and enter its identification letter in the space provided:

____ 1. Examples of committed fixed costs could include: (a) direct labor wages, (b) bond interest expense, (c) management training costs, (d) none of these.

____ 2. Examples of step-function costs could include: (a) salaries of billing clerks, (b) research and development costs, (c) direct materials used, (d) none of these.

____ 3. Examples of discretionary fixed costs could include: (a) sales commissions, (b) fire insurance on factory building, (c) salaries of payroll clerks, (d) annual factory picnic and holiday party.

____ 4. Examples of strictly variable costs could include: (a) plant manager's salary, (b) wages of maintenance personnel, (c) heating and air conditioning costs, (d) none of these.

____ 5. Costs that can usually be evaluated most reliably in terms of the benefits they generate are: (a) discretionary variable costs, (b) discretionary fixed costs, (c) committed fixed costs, (d) engineered variable costs.

____ 6. Cost prediction methods that use all data

points include: (a) least-squares method, (b) visual-fit method, (c) both of these, (d) neither of these.

____ 7. Once capital expenditures are made, the basic control approach for the resultant fixed costs is to increase the current utilization of the facilities: (a) true, (b) false.

____ 8. Discretionary fixed costs stem from periodic appropriation decisions that directly reflect top management policies: (a) true, (b) false.

____ 9. Discretionary fixed costs are also called: (a) programmed costs, (b) managed costs, (c) both of these, (d) neither of these.

____ 10. In contrast to discretionary fixed costs, committed fixed costs are: (a) more difficult to measure and evaluate in terms of their outputs, (b) less easily influenced by management on a short-term basis, (c) both of these, (d) neither of these.

____ 11. Costs that are generally most likely to behave as engineered variable costs are: (a) advertising, (b) direct labor, (c) research and development, (d) direct materials.

____ 12. The work-measurement approach to cost control is conceptually: (a) a discretionary-cost approach, (b) an informal approach, (c) a variable-cost approach, (d) none of these.

___ 13. An example (or examples) of a **control-factor unit** for use in a work-measurement approach to controlling costs of preparing customer invoices would include: (a) number of billing clerks, (b) number of invoice lines per hour, (c) both of these, (d) neither of these.

___ 14. See the preceding test item. The **perfection standard** for the work would be: (a) the total number of invoices to be prepared per month by all billing clerks, (b) the number of billing clerks to be used per month, (c) both of these, (d) neither of these.

___ 15. The approach actually used by most organizations in controlling their nonmanufacturing costs is: (a) a work-measurement approach, (b) a variable-cost approach, (c) a discretionary-cost approach, (d) none of these.

___ 16. The cost-control approach that views nonmanufacturing costs as fixed costs is: (a) a formal approach, (b) a work-measurement approach, (c) a discretionary-cost approach, (d) none of these.

___ 17. Zero-base budgeting pertains primarily to: (a) variable costs, (b) committed costs, (c) discretionary costs.

___ 18. The incremental approach is used by: (a) traditional budgeting, (b) zero-base budgeting, (c) both traditional and zero-base budgeting, (d) neither traditional nor zero-base budgeting.

___ 19. Managerial accountants commonly assume that an adequate explanation of cost behavior requires: (a) only one independent variable, (b) several independent variables, (c) one or more dependent variables.

___ 20. In general, managerial accountants assume that cost behavior can be reflected satisfactorily: (a) by linear cost functions, (b) only by nonlinear cost functions.

___ 21. The budgeted annual cost of operating a post-office truck is $4,400 plus 20¢ per mile. In 19X2 the truck was to be used for 20,000 miles. If these data were reflected in a linear equation to represent the cost function, the **independent variable** would be: (a) $4,400, (b) 20¢, (c) 20,000 miles, (d) $8,400, (e) some other figure.

___ 22. See the preceding test item. The **dependent variable** would be: (a), (b), (c), (d), (e).

___ 23. See item 21 above. The **intercept** would be: (a), (b), (c), (d), (e).

___ 24. In general, our search for appropriate cost functions places primary emphasis on: (a) economic plausibility, (b) goodness of fit, (c) both of these, (d) neither of these.

___ 25. The inclusion of fixed- and variable-cost elements in one ledger account is: (a) ideally appropriate, (b) seldom seen in practice, (c) both of these, (d) neither of these.

___ 26. The monthly building maintenance expense of a company was $43,000 when direct-labor hours were 2,000 and $38,500 when direct labor-hours were 1,700. The indicated fixed cost per month was: (a) $13,000, (b) $23,000, (c) $33,000, (d) some other amount.

___ 27. See the preceding test item. The indicated variable-cost rate per labor-hour was: (a) $6.50, (b) $15.00, (c) $5.00, (d) some other rate.

II Complete each of the following statements:

1. The two major types of variable costs are _____ _____ costs and _____ costs.

2. Variable costs that may fluctuate with sales merely because management has allocated in advance certain proportions of dollar sales are called _____ costs.

3. Standards used in work measurement are in terms of _____ units needed for a given quantity of some specified work.

4. The cost-control approach that views nonman-ufacturing costs as variable costs is called _____ _____ .

5. Cost-behavior patterns may also be called _____ .

III Dickenson Company employs six billing clerks at a salary of $2,000 per month each. Each clerk is supposed to process 4,000 invoices per month. In April, 23,000 invoices were processed. Compute:

1. Actual cost .... $ _____

2. Flexible-budget cost .... $ _____

3. Budget variance .... $ _____

IV Solari Instruments, Inc. uses an equation for predicting the annual cost of operating its delivery trucks: y = $28,000 + 20¢ x.

1. Identify or determine the symbol or amount that represents each of the following ideas or amounts:

   (a) The dependent variable .... $ _____

   (b) The independent variable .... $ _____

   (c) The slope of the regression line .... $ _____

   (d) The total cost if x is 200,000 .... $ _____

   (e) The mathematical value of the dependent variable when the independent variable is zero .... $ _____

2. See (e).
Is this the expected cost at zero activity? _____

Why? _____

_____

V Given for a certain mixed factory overhead cost of Frishkoff Company:

	50,000	60,000
Volume of activity in direct labor-hours per month	50,000	60,000
Total cost per month	$14,000	$16,200

1. Compute the variable-cost rate per direct labor-hour .... $ _____

2. Compute the indicated fixed cost per month .... $ _____

3. Express the cost behavior pattern in formula form:

CHAPTER 8 SOLUTIONS TO PRACTICE TEST QUESTIONS AND PROBLEMS

I

1 b	5 d	9 c	13 b	17 c	21 c	25 d
2 a	6 c	10 b	14 d	18 a	22 d	26 a
3 d	7 a	11 d	15 c	19 a	23 a	27 b
4 d	8 a	12 c	16 c	20 a	24 c	

Computations:

22 $4,400 + (20¢)(20,000) = \$4,400 + \$4,000 = \$8,400$ (d)

26 $43,000 − \$38,500 = \$4,500; 2,000 − 1,700 = 300$ hours;
$\$4,500 ÷ 300 = \$15$ per hour variable-cost rate;
$\$43,000 − (\$15)(2,000) = \$43,000 − \$30,000 = \$13,000$ (a);
or $\$38,500 − (\$15)(1,700) = \$38,500 − \$25,500 = \$13,000$

27 See 26, $15 (b)

II 1 engineered and discretionary, 2 discretionary variable, 3 control-factor, 4 work measurement, 5 cost functions.

III Dickenson Company

1. $6 \times 2,000 = \$12,000$
2. $2,000 ÷ 4,000 = \$.50$ per invoice; $23,000 \times \$.50 = \$11,500$
3. $\$12,000 − \$11,500 = \$500$ unfavorable

IV Solari Instruments, Inc.

1. (a) y; (b) x; (c) 20¢; (d) $y = \$28,000 + (20¢)(200,000) = \$68,000$; (e) $y = \$28,000 + (20¢)(0) = \$28,000$
2. no

Although a cost function estimated for a mixed cost (as in this case) may yield a good approximation to the actual cost function over the relevant range, such a relevant range rarely includes zero activity. Therefore the **intercept** ($28,000 in this case) would probably not be the expected cost at zero activity because the actual observations probably did not include the point where activity was zero and the cost function was probably not linear beyond the relevant range.

V Frishkoff Company

1. Variable rate $= \dfrac{\text{Change in mixed cost}}{\text{Change in volume}} = \dfrac{\$16,200 − \$14,000}{60,000 − 50,000}$
$= \dfrac{\$2,200}{10,000} = \$.22$ per direct labor hour
2. Fixed component = Total mixed cost less variable component:
At 60,000-hour level $= \$16,200 − \$.22(60,000) = \$3,000$
Or, 50,000-hour level $= \$14,000 − \$.22(50,000) = \$3,000$
3. Cost formula $= \$3,000$ per month $+ \$.22$ per direct labor hour.

Chapter 9

RESPONSIBILITY ACCOUNTING AND
COST ALLOCATION

MAIN FOCUS AND OBJECTIVES

The design of a successful management accounting system rests on a few main ideas:

- *Collective management decisions must lead to organization goals.*
- *Performance measurement greatly influences management decisions.*
- *A responsibility-center structure should identify managerial authority and performance.*

This chapter focuses on the principal elements of a responsibility accounting system with particular emphasis upon:

- *devices and techniques for controlling costs*
- *effects of cost allocations on management behavior*

REVIEW OF KEY IDEAS

A. Responsibility centers correspond to the usual delegation of decision making within an organization.
   1. Principal forms:
      a. **Cost centers,** usually departments for which costs are accumulated and reported.
      b. **Profit centers,** usually divisions that are responsible for both revenues and expenses.
      c. **Investment centers,** which are responsible for their invested capital as well as for revenues and expenses.
   2. **Responsibility performance reports** provide managers of responsibility centers on each level with data concerning the items they have the authority and ability to influence.

3. Such reports show budgeted amounts of revenues and expenses and the variances of actual amounts from the budget.
   a. This focus on the variances illustrates **management by exception.**
   b. Managers thus need not waste their time and effort on those parts of the report that reflect the smoothly running phases of operations.
4. A responsibility accounting system obviously can facilitate the delegation of decision making.
   a. In addition, the performance reports of the system generate useful data for evaluating managers and thus tend to improve their efforts toward organization goals.
   b. Therefore, such reports often identify or exclude any expenses **beyond the control** of the manager being evaluated.

B. The key idea in a responsibility accounting system is the **controllability of costs.**
   1. A **controllable cost** is a cost that can be influenced by a given **manager** of a given **responsibility center** for a given period of **time.**
      a. Controllability is a matter of degree.
      b. For example, more costs are controllable at higher levels within an organization and/or as the time span increases.

> **Question: Does a responsibility accounting system aim at placing blame or finding fault?**
> **Answer: No. See below.**

   2. In many situations, a manager may have only a little influence over operating results.
      a. Nevertheless, a responsibility accounting system must identify the person with the most day-to-day influence over a particular cost or revenue.
      b. That person will then at least be responsible for **explaining deviations** of actual results from budgeted results.

C. The assignment of costs to cost objectives is called **cost allocation.**
   1. The basic conceptual approach of cost allocation is twofold:
      a. Group like costs together in a **pool.**
      b. Identify each cost pool with one or more **cost objectives** via an **allocation base** that plausibly links costs with objectives.
   2. Basic types of cost allocations:
      a. Allocation to responsibility centers
      b. Reallocation from one center to other centers
      c. Allocation to products or services
   3. Major purposes of cost allocation:
      a. To predict the economic effects of planning and control decisions
      b. To promote goal congruence and managerial effort, and thus to obtain desired motivation of managers.
      c. To measure costs and profits of individual products and projects
      d. To help determine output prices that are based on costs

D. Many organizations allocate costs to organization segments by combining a responsibility accounting system with the **contribution approach.**

See textbook Exhibit 9-4

1. This is a model income statement by segments at three different segment levels: branches, product lines, and individual stores.
2. Note carefully that this report attempts to report costs by **controllability** as well as by **behavior pattern.**
3. The resulting amounts are therefore generally useful for evaluating performance and making planning decisions.
4. The **segmented contribution margins** (excess of revenues over allocable variable costs) are helpful in predicting the impact on income of short-run changes in volume (line *a* in Exhibit 9-4).
5. The **contribution controllable by segment managers** may be computed as the excess of segment contribution margins over the fixed costs controllable by segment managers (line *b* in Exhibit 9-4).
6. However, the performance of a division (or other segment) as an **economic investment** is measured only after a further deduction for allocable fixed costs controllable by others, which leaves a remainder called **contribution by segments** (line *c* of Exhibit 9-4).

> **Question: If a cost cannot be allocated to certain segments on a meaningful basis, should it be included in the income statement?**
>
> **Answer: Yes, but it should be clearly identified as not allocated with respect to those segments. See the $20 and $30 items below line *a* in Exhibit 9-4.**

E. Guidelines for allocating service department costs:
  1. Divide the costs of a particular service department into **two pools:** variable and fixed.
  2. Allocate the **variable-cost pool** to other segments by multiplying the **budgeted usage rate** by the **actual volume of usage.**
     a. The use of predetermined cost rates protects the using departments from operational inefficiences of service departments and subsequent price changes.
     b. Thus, allocations are more likely to be viewed by managers as fair and will be less likely to cause undesirable motivational effects.
  3. Allocate the **fixed-cost pool** to other segments by multiplying the **budgeted total fixed costs** by the **budgeted proportions of capacity available to users.**
     a. This predetermined **lump-sum** allocation prevents the allocations to user departments from being affected by the actual usage of other departments.
     b. Thus, motivational effects of allocation are more likely to be positive.

F. Organizations typically incur many **central costs** such as expenses of corporate headquarters and various company-wide expenses.
  1. Because of the lack of a plausible allocation scheme, many companies do not allocate such costs.
  2. However, if these costs are to be allocated, an undesirable motivational effect can usually be avoided by using the same approach described in E3 above for allocating the fixed costs of a service department.

G. An important purpose for allocating costs is to determine costs to be used as a basis for pricing outputs of tangible products or intangible services.

1. There are two principal techniques for allocating service department costs to revenue or production departments.
2. The **direct method** allocates no service department costs to other service departments.
   a. This method directly transfers **all** service department costs to the revenue departments.
   b. The bases for these allocations are the **relative measures** of services received only by the revenue departments, as indicated in the important footnotes of Exhibit 9-7.
3. The **step-down method** does allocate service department costs to other service departments.
   a. However, once a service department's cost is transferred out, no other costs are transferred back to it.
   b. You should carefully study the computations of allocated costs, as shown in the footnotes to Exhibit 9-7.
4. Note how the rates are developed for **applying costs to outputs** (the last line of each of the two sections of Exhibit 9-7).

PRACTICE TEST QUESTIONS AND PROBLEMS WITH SOLUTIONS

I For each of the following multiple-choice and true-false statements, select the most appropriate answer and enter its identification letter in the space provided:

____ 1. Managers are expected to take risks even though they may have limited control over outcomes: (a) true, (b) false.

____ 2. Responsibility accounting basically asks, "Which individual in the organization is in the best position to: (a) control the outcome, (b) explain why the outcome occurred, (c) predict the outcome, (d) take the blame for the outcome."

____ 3. Profit centers cannot exist in nonprofit organizations: (a) true, (b) false.

____ 4. The focus of responsibility accounting is: (a) accounting accuracy, (b) rewarding managers, (c) identifying blame or fault, (d) information gathering.

____ 5. The direct method of allocating service department costs ignores all services rendered by service departments to other service departments: (a) true, (b) false.

____ 6. The smallest segment of activity or area of responsibility for which costs are accumulated is called: (a) a mini center, (b) a profit center, (c) a cost center, (d) an investment center.

____ 7. Managers should focus their attention on the parts of performance reports that do not reflect smoothly running aspects of operations. This is called: (a) exceptional management, (b) management by perception, (c) perceptional management, (d) management by exception.

____ 8. The **major** purposes of cost allocation include: (a) obtaining a basis for setting output prices, (b) measuring income and asset valuations, (c) aiding in making planning and control decisions, (d) all of these, (e) none of these.

____ 9. A contribution income statement by segments is aimed at reporting costs by: (a) their behavioral pattern, (b) their controllability, (c) both of these, (d) neither of these.

____ 10. If a cost cannot be allocated to certain segments on a meaningful basis, it should be: (a) excluded from the income statement, (b) included in the income statement but not allocated.

11. The segment **contribution margins** are most helpful in measuring: (a) long-run segment profitability, (b) short-run performance of division managers or product managers, (c) effects on segment net income of long-run changes in the volume, (d) long-run earning power of the entire company.

12. Net income before income taxes is the total contribution by segments less unallocated costs: (a) true, (b) false.

13. The following data in thousands appeared for a certain segment of a company in the contribution-approach income statement: variable expenses $500, fixed costs controllable by others $80, fixed costs controllable by segment managers $110, net sales $690. The contribution margin is: (a) zero, (b) $640, (c) $190, (d) $580, (e) $80.

14. See the preceding test item. The contribution controllable by segment managers is: (a), (b), (c), (d), (e).

15. Usually, the same criteria should be used in evaluating the performance of a division as an **investment by the company** and the **performance of a division manager:** (a) true, (b) false.

16. Ram Co. prepared a contribution-margin income statement that included the following data in thousands for one of its segments: fixed costs controllable by segment managers $240, fixed costs controllable by others $150, variable expenses $300, net sales $750. The economic performance of the segment is measured best by: (a) $60, (b) $210, (c) $450, (d) $540.

17. A service department in a large company presents the following data: budgeted variable costs per direct labor-hour $1.50; actual direct labor-hours: 8,000 for Producing Dept. A, 12,000 for B; budgeted labor-hours: for A 9,000, for B 11,000; long-run expected direct-labor hours: for A 11,000, for B 9,000. Compute the allocation of variable costs to A if actual variable costs are $40,000: (a) $16,000, (b) $12,000, (c) $18,000, (d) $13,500, (e) $22,000, (f) 16,500.

18. In order to prevent the variable-cost charges to a given operating department from being distorted by changes in the costs or efficiencies of service departments, one can use allocation rates based on: (a) actual hours and costs, (b) predetermined hours and costs.

19. The long-run demand hours of Producing Department A-5 are 10% of the capacity of a certain service department, but A-5 actually used 20% of the output of the service department during a certain period. The budgeted fixed costs of the service department for that period were $90,000, but the actual fixed costs were $100,000. The allocation of fixed costs to A-5 should be: (a) 10% of $90,000, (b) 10% of $100,000, (c) 20% of $90,000, (d) 20% of $100,000.

20. The capacity or peak needs of operating or producing departments would provide the most suitable base for allocating: (a) total power costs, (b) the variable element of power costs, (c) the fixed element of power costs.

21. The step-down method of allocating service department costs ignores: (a) **all** services rendered by service departments to other service departments, (b) the **reciprocal** services among service departments, (c) both of these, (d) neither of these.

22. Service Departments A and B each has $80,000 of overhead to be allocated. They render 20% of their services to each other. Producing Department C receives 10% of the service of A and 30% of the service of B. Use the step-down method to compute the total overhead to be allocated to C from A and B. Begin with Department B. (a) $32,000, (b) $40,000, (c) $34,000, (d) $36,000.

23. Service Department P has $70,000 of overhead to be allocated. It renders 30% of its service to other service departments, 10% to Producing Department Q, and the remainder to all the other pro-

ducing departments. The cost to be allocated from P to Q by the direct method is: (a) $7,000, (b) $11,667, (c) $4,900, (d) none of these.

_____ 24. Acceptable ways of dealing with the central costs of an organization include: (a) not allocating to organization segments, (b) allocating by a variable-cost approach, (c) either of these, (d) neither of these.

II Complete each of the following statements:

1. A convincing or plausible link between costs and cost objectives is called a _____ .

2. Before allocating costs, one should usually group like costs into _____ .

3. The contribution margin by segments is _____ _____ less _____ _____ .

4. The contribution controllable by division managers is the excess of the _____ _____ margin over the fixed _____ _____ .

5. The contribution by segments is the excess of the contribution _____ _____ over the fixed costs _____ .

6. In the allocation of costs of such services as power, the variable-cost element may be distributed by a _____ _____ and the fixed cost element may be distributed as _____ _____ .

7. In order to prevent the fixed-cost charges to a given operating department from depending on the quantity of services actually consumed by other operating departments, one can use allocation amounts based on _____ _____ hours and costs.

III From the following data for Specific Equipment Company, prepare a contribution approach income statement by segments:

(In thousands of dollars)	Company Total	Beta Division	Gamma Division
Net sales	$850	$500	$350
Fixed costs:			
Controllable by division managers	140	60	80
Controllable by others	70	10	60
Variable costs:			
Manufacturing cost of sales	450	300	150
Selling and administrative expenses	130	60	70
Unallocated costs	45	—	—

	Company Total	Beta Division	Gamma Division

IV Reagan Company's power plant provides electricity for its two producing departments, X and Y. The 19X3 budget for the power plant shows:

Budgeted fixed costs	$70.000
Budgeted variable costs per kilowatt hour (KWH)	$ 0.15

Additional data for 19X3:

	Dept. X	Dept. Y
Long-run demand (KWH)	420,000	280,000
Budgeted for 19X3 (KWH)	310,000	200,000
Actual for 19X3 (KWH)	320,000	160,000

Actual power plant costs for 19X3 are:

Fixed .... $78,000;   Variable $81,000

Compute the 19X3 allocation of power plant costs to Departments X and Y:

	1. Fixed	2. Variable
Dept. X	$ _____	$ _____
Dept. Y	$ _____	$ _____

V Expert Innovations, Inc. provides the following information:

	Service Dept. 1	Service Dept. 2	Production Dept. X	All Other Production Depts.
Overhead costs before allocation	$4,000	$4,500	$5,000	$51,000
Proportions of service furnished by Dept. 1	—	20%	30%	50%
Proportions of service furnished by Dept. 2	10%	—	40%	50%

1. Use the **direct method** to allocate costs and determine the total overhead of Dept. X after allocation.

	Dept. 1	Dept. 2	Dept. X	Others
Overhead costs before allocation	$4,000	$4,500	$5,000	$51,000

2. Use the **step-down method** to allocate costs and determine the total overhead of Dept. X after allocation. **Begin with Dept. 2.**

	Dept. 1	Dept. 2	Dept. X	Others
Overhead costs before allocation	$4,000	$4,500	$5,000	$51,000

I					
1 a	5 a	9 c	13 c	17 b	21 b
2 b	6 c	10 b	14 e	18 b	22 d
3 b	7 d	11 b	15 b	19 a	23 d
4 d	8 d	12 a	16 a	20 c	24 a

Computations:

13 $690 − $500 = $190 (c)
14 $690 − $500 − $110 = $80 (e)
16 $750 − $300 − $240 − $150 = $60 (a)
17 $1.50 × 8,000 = $12,000 (b)
22 (d)

	A	B	C	Others
Overhead	$ 80,000	$ 80,000		
Allocate B (.2, .3, .5)	16,000	(80,000)	$24,000	$ 40,000
Allocate A ($\frac{1}{8}, \frac{7}{8}$)*	$(96,000)		12,000	84,000
Totals			$36,000	$124,000

Proof: 80,000 + 80,000 = 36,000 + 124,000 = 160,000

*10% ÷ (10% + 70%) = $\frac{1}{8}$; 70% ÷ (10% + 70%) = $\frac{7}{8}$
23 100% − 30% = 70%; 10% ÷ 70% = $\frac{1}{7}$; $70,000 ÷ 7 = $10,000 (d)

II   1 cost allocation base, 2 cost pools, 3 net sales less variable costs, 4 contribution margin over the fixed costs controllable by division (or segment) managers, 5 controllable by segment (or division) managers over the fixed costs controllable by others, 6 budgeted (or standard) rate per unit of services consumed, lump-sum predetermined monthly charges, 7 predetermined (or budgeted).

III   Specific Equipment Company

	Company Total	Beta Division	Gamma Division
Net sales	$850	$500	$350
Less variable costs:			
Manufacturing cost of sales	$450	$300	$150
Variable selling and administrative expenses	130	60	70
Total variable costs	$580	$360	$220
(a) Contribution margin	$270	$140	$130
Less fixed costs controllable by division			
managers	140	60	80
(b) Contribution controllable by division managers	$130	$ 80	$ 50
Less fixed costs controllable by others	70	10	60
(c) Contribution by segments	$ 60	$ 70	$(10)
Less unallocated costs	45		
(d) Income before income taxes	$ 15		

IV   Reagan Company

1. Use long-run demand to allocate budgeted fixed costs
   (total KWH: 420,000 + 280,000 = 700,000):
   Dept. X: (420,000/700,000) × $70,000 = $42,000
   Dept. Y: (280,000/700,000) × $70,000 = $28,000
2. Use predetermined rates and actual KWH to allocate variable costs:
   Dept. X: 15¢ × 320,000 = $48,000
   Dept. Y: 15¢ × 160,000 = $24,000
   (Unallocated actual costs for 19X3 may be written off to expense at end of year.)

V   Expert Innovations, Inc.

	Dept. 1	Dept. 2	Dept. X	Others
1. Overhead costs before allocation	$ 4,000	$ 4,500	$5,000	$51,000
Dept. 1 costs allocated, $\frac{3}{8}$ and $\frac{5}{8}$	($4,000)	—	1,500	2,500
Dept. 2 costs allocated, $\frac{4}{9}$ and $\frac{5}{9}$		(4,500)	2,000	2,500
Totals			$8,500	$56,000
2. Overhead costs before allocation	$ 4,000	$ 4,500	$5,000	$51,000
Dept. 2 costs allocated, 10%, 40%, 50%	450	(4,500)	1,800	2,250
Dept. 1 costs allocated, $\frac{3}{8}$ and $\frac{5}{8}$	(4,450)	—	1,669	2,781
Totals			$8,469	$56,031

Chapter 10

PROFIT CENTERS AND
TRANSFER PRICING

MAIN FOCUS AND OBJECTIVES

To complete the basic description of management control systems, this chapter covers two closely related areas:

- *Criteria for evaluating control systems*
- *Ways to measure performance in decentralized organizations*

The first area includes *goal congruence* and *managerial effort*, that is, inducing managers to embrace organizational goals and work energetically toward them.

The second area assumes an environment of *decentralization*, which is the freedom of decision making at subunit levels. We focus on the key aids in measuring the performance of organization segments:

- *Transfer prices*
- *Rate of return on investment*
- *Residual income*

REVIEW OF KEY IDEAS

A. Criteria for designing and evaluating a control system:
1. Weighing of **costs** against **benefits.**
2. Achievement of **goal congruence;** managers must perceive that their own best interests harmonize with the overall objectives of top management.
3. Obtaining **energetic managerial effort** toward organization goals.
4. In sum, the management accounting systems and methods should have a **behavioral focus;** they should be designed to promote **motivation:** the need to achieve organization goals and the drive toward those goals.

B. Decentralization:

1. **Definition:** the delegation of freedom to segment managers for making decisions.
2. **Benefits:**
   a. Better and more timely decisions because of managers' proximity to local conditions
   b. Improvement of managerial skills by a wider distribution of decision making
   c. Motivational increase from enhanced status of managers
3. **Costs:**
   a. Dysfunctional effects caused by narrow focus on segment performance and unawareness of all relevant information
   b. Costly duplication of central services
   c. Increased costs of gathering and processing data for numerous segment managers
4. Decentralization tends to be most successful when segments are relatively **independent** of each other.
5. An additional criterion for designing and evaluating a control system is **segment autonomy.**
   a. This means allowing segment managers to make decisions without interference from top managers.

6.
> **Question: Is decentralization equivalent to the use of profit centers?**
> **Answer: No. One can exist without the other. See below.**

   a. **Decentralization** is the delegation of the freedom to make decisions.
   b. **Profit centers** account for revenues and expenses of segments.
   c. Thus, profit centers are devices that can **aid decentralization.**

C. Transfer pricing necessarily results from the exchanges of goods and services among the decentralized segments of a company.

1. Transfer prices are the monetary values assigned to these exchanges or transfers.
2. Actually, transfer pricing is a form of **cost allocation.**
3. The purpose of transfer pricing is to help the organization operate more efficiently and more effectively. This purpose rests on the same criteria for designing and evaluating control systems.
4. No single type of transfer price is universally applicable.
5. Using **total actual cost** is generally not recommended.
   a. It fails to provide the buying segment with a reliable basis for planning.
   b. It fails to provide the supplying segment with appropriate incentive for controlling its costs.
   c. **Budgeted or standard costs** would be more beneficial as transfer prices (allocation bases), as pointed out in the preceding chapter.
6. Using **market prices** for transfer prices is often appropriate when an organization has profit centers.
   a. The problems of goal congruence, managerial effort, and segment autonomy are minimized.
   b. If market prices do not exist or cannot be determined, a substitute base may be used: "cost-plus-a-profit."
7. Using **variable cost** for transfer prices can induce decisions that benefit the organization.

    a. If the producing division **has no idle capacity,** using **market price** as a transfer price would result in the correct decision to **sell to outsiders.**

    b. However, if the producing division **does have idle capacity,** the use of **variable cost** as a transfer price would cause the correct decision to **sell to another division** for processing before sale to outsiders.

8. To avoid the **dysfunctional behavior** that could result from a strict use of a single type of transfer price, a superior manager could, in certain situations, designate a particular transfer price at which the transfer must be made.

    a. This procedure assumes the risk of **undermining segment autonomy.**

    b. Therefore it might be better to offer special incentives to induce goal congruent behavior.

9. A given company may well choose to use different transfer prices for different purposes: motivation, performance measurement, taxation, and government regulation.

D. The measures of accomplishment that best represent the objectives of top management usually relate profits to **invested capital.**

1. A widely used measure is the **rate of return on investment (ROI).**

    a. ROI can be computed as:

$$\frac{\text{Income}}{\text{Invested capital}}$$

    b. Alternative computation:

$$\textbf{(Income percentage of revenue)} \times \textbf{(Capital turnover)} = \textbf{ROI}$$

$$\left(\frac{\textbf{Income}}{\textbf{Revenue}}\right) \times \left(\frac{\textbf{Revenue}}{\textbf{Capital}}\right) = \frac{\textbf{Income}}{\textbf{Capital}}$$

    c. Management's understanding and use of the rate of return in (a) above are aided by subdividing it into its basic components as shown in (b). For example, the rate of return may be improved by reducing expenses or reducing investment in assets.

2. **Residual income (RI)** is another important measure of accomplishment that relates profit to invested capital.

    a. This is the **excess of income over the imputed interest on average capital invested.**

    b. This approach induces a desirable expansion of an investment center as long as it earns a rate in excess of the charge for invested capital (the minimum desired rate of return).

    c. In contrast to the results of the residual income approach, using the maximization of ROI as an investment criterion would sometimes result in the rejection by division managers of projects that, from the viewpoint of the organizations, should be accepted because they promise an ROI in excess of the minimum desired rate of return.

3. However, either an ROI or an RI system can promote goal congruence and incentive if a **budget** is properly used as a focus for effort.

4. In measuring performance by whatever means, one should make a distinction between the performance of the **division manager** and the performance of the **division as an investment** by the corporation.

    a. To measure divisional performance, one could appropriately compare division income with the **total** division investment.

b. On the other hand, a division manager's performance would be more appropriately evaluated by comparing the income of the manager's division with only the investment **controllable by the manager.**

E. The budget always plays a key role in an effective management control system.
   1. Management by objectives (MBO) involves the joint formulation by manager and superior of a set of goals and achievement plans for a forthcoming period.
      a. The plans may consist mainly of a responsibility accounting budget.
      b. The budget is focused on currently attainable results and thus should clearly identify costs within each manager's control.
   2. The budget should be tailored to the needs of particular managers so as to maximize goal congruence and incentive.

F. In designing performance measures, one should be aware of different definitions of key elements and their implications for appraising performance and motivating managers.
   1. Various definitions of **income** for the segments of an organization were presented in the preceding chapter.
   2. Different bases can be used for measuring **invested capital.**
      a. In general, for evaluating the **operating performance of managers,** it is appropriate to use as a base an asset total **not reduced by any long-term debt.**
      b. Such bases include **total assets, total assets employed,** and **total assets less current liabilities.**
      c. The use of **stockholders' equity** (total assets less all liabilities) would usually not be appropriate, because division managers typically have little responsibility for the **long-term portion** of liabilities associated with the assets they use.
   3. The method of **allocating asset costs** to divisions can significantly affect the motivation of managers.
      a. A common criterion for allocation is the amount of assets the company could **avoid** by not having that particular division.
      b. Many managers feel it is better **not** to allocate asset costs to divisions than to use an **arbitrary** basis for allocation.
   4. Of crucial importance is the **valuation base** for measuring assets.
      a. For the routine measurement of assets included in the investment base, the most frequently used valuation is **historical cost** because it is generally believed that its use for this purpose may be more economical than the use of replacement and disposal values, which are often viewed as not feasible to obtain except for special decisions.
      b. When historical cost is used as an investment measure, some users prefer **gross book value** (undepreciated cost) because it facilitates comparisons among divisions, but others prefer **net book value** (cost less accumulated depreciation) because it is consistent with conventional reporting of assets and net income.

PRACTICE TEST QUESTIONS AND PROBLEMS WITH SOLUTIONS

I For each of the following multiple-choice and true-false statements, select the most appropriate answer and enter its identification letter in the space provided:

____ 1. The internal control system requirements of the U.S. Foreign Corrupt Practices Act: (a) are the nucleus of management control systems, (b) are concerned with transaction errors and other accounting matters, (c) pertain primarily to companies with significant foreign trade, (d) pertain primarily to budgets and planning matters.

____ 2. The main criteria for designing and evaluating control systems include: (a) managerial effort, (b) segment autonomy, (c) both of these, (d) none of these.

3. Decentralization tends to be most successful when the segments of an organization are relatively interdependent: (a) true, (b) false.

4. The existence of an organization's decentralization depends on the existence of profit centers within the organization: (a) true, (b) false.

5. Segment autonomy means the freedom of each organization segment to define its job or function: (a) true, (b) false.

6. The costs of decentralization can include: (a) poorer training for managers, (b) dysfunctional decision making, (c) both of these, (d) neither of these.

7. The benefits of decentralization can include: (a) improved management motivation, (b) decreased costs of gathering and processing information, (c) both of these, (d) neither of these.

8. Transfer pricing is a form of: (a) transportation charge, (b) cost allocation, (c) price bargaining, (d) profit planning.

9. Disadvantages of transfer prices based on total actual cost include: (a) reduction of incentive of managers of supplying divisions to control their costs, (b) failure to furnish the buying segment with a reliable basis for planning, (c) both of these, (d) neither of these.

10. The Red division of Hue Co. has an idle capacity of 1,000 units per month for producing an element that it usually makes at a unit cost of $120 variable and $80 fixed. If another division of Hue were to buy 1,000 units of the same element at a market price of $130 from an outside supplier, there would be a per-unit advantage to Hue of: (a) $10, (b) $70, (c) neither of these, but a disadvantage.

11. See the preceding test item. If the element were to be purchased on the outside at a market price of $110, there would be a per-unit advantage to Hue of: (a) $10,

(b) $90, (c) neither of these, but a disadvantage.

12. The correct internal buy-sell decision based on transfer prices at variable cost is more likely when the producing division: (a) has idle capacity, (b) has no idle capacity.

13. The most likely basis for transfer prices when an organization has profit centers is: (a) full cost, (b) variable cost, (c) market price.

14. When full costs are used as transfer prices, an incentive to control the inefficiencies that might increase such costs would be provided by using: (a) full actual costs, (b) full standard costs.

15. Agency theory pertains to: (a) choices of performance measures and rewards, (b) delegation of authority by top management, (c) functions of profit centers, (d) relationship of employees to their organization.

16. The critical test of the profitability of an organization is: (a) the absolute amount of profit, (b) the relationship of profit to sales, (c) the relationship of profit to the number of employees, (d) the relationship of profit to invested capital.

17. An investment center is a business segment that relates its net income to its: (a) sales, (b) liabilities, (c) stockholders, (d) invested capital.

18. ROI is income percentage of revenue multiplied by: (a) sales, (b) income, (c) capital turnover, (d) total assets.

19. Given for a division of Bugatti Co.: 18% ROI, 6% operating income on revenues, and $2 million of invested capital. Compute total revenues: (a) $360,000, (b) $6 million, (c) $120,000, (d) none of these.

20. Given for a division of Raven Co.: $32,000 operating income, $800,000 revenues, and a capital turnover of five times. Compute ROI: (a) 4%, (b) 5%, (c) 10%, (d) none of these.

21. Olivier Corporation turned its capital six times and earned an operating income of

2.5% of sales. Compute ROI: (a) 6%, (b) .4%, (c) 15%, (d) none of these.

___ 22. Other factors remaining the same, the rate of return on investment may be improved by: (a) increasing investment in assets, (b) increasing expenses, (c) reducing sales, (d) decreasing investment in assets.

___ 23. Residual income is the excess of an investment center's income over: (a) operating expenses, (b) dividends to stockholders, (c) imputed interest on average capital invested.

___ 24. An analytical approach that tends to cause a desirable expansion of an investment center as long as it earns a rate in excess of the charge for invested capital is: (a) the residual-income approach, (b) the ROI approach, (c) either of these, (d) neither of these.

___ 25. Mas Co. has $10 million of operating assets and an operating income of $2 million. What is residual income if imputed interest is 14%? (a) none, (b) $400,000, (c) $600,000, (d) some other amount.

___ 26. If the investment criterion is the maximization of rate of return on investment, division managers will sometimes reject projects that, for the welfare of the total organization, should be accepted: (a) true, (b) false.

___ 27. It is better to: (a) use an arbitrary basis for allocating asset costs to divisions, (b) not allocate asset costs to divisions.

___ 28. In general, for evaluating the operating performance of managers, it is appropriate to use as an investment base: (a) an asset total reduced by long-term debt, (b) an asset total not reduced by long-term debt.

___ 29. The use of stockholders' equity as an investment base would be quite appropriate for evaluating: (a) owners' returns, (b) management performance, (c) both of these, (d) neither of these.

___ 30. When historical cost is used as an investment measure, it is more appropriate to use: (a) gross book value, (b) net book value.

___ 31. Control systems in nonprofit organizations will never be as highly developed as in profit-seeking organizations because: (a) there is no business competition and therefore less need for information, (b) the average ability of personnel tends to be lower in nonprofit organizations, (c) in nonprofit organizations, goals are less clear and it is harder to measure results in meaningful terms.   \

II Complete each of the following statements:

1. When approaches are used to help produce management decisions that will lead to the achievement of organizational goals, this state or relationship is called _____.

2. Desirable motivation within an organization is a combination of _____ and _____.

3. Decentralization of an organization is defined as _____ _____.

4. Transfer pricing systems are aimed at meeting four criteria: (a) cost-benefit trade-offs, (b) goal _____, (c) _____ _____, and (d) _____.

5. A strict use of a single type of transfer price within an organization could produce _____ _____ behavior.

6. ROI is _____ divided by _____.

7. Capital turnover is _____ divided by _____.

8. The most frequently used valuation basis for measuring assets included in the investment base for rate of return is _____.

III Given for three divisions of Unique Brands Inc.:

	Maritime Division	Farm Division	Industrial Division
Invested capital	$250,000	$200,000	*
Revenues (sales)	750,000	*	$450,000
Net income	37,500	*	$ 13,500
Capital turnover	*	*	4.5 times
Income percentage of revenue	*	5%	*
Rate of return on investment	*	10%	*

*Figures to be computed

1. Find for the Maritime Division:

   (a) Capital turnover .... _____ times

   (b) Income percentage of revenues .... _____ %

   (c) Rate of return on investment .... _____ %

2. Find for the Farm Division:

   (a) Net income .... $ _____

   (b) Revenues .... $ _____

   (c) Capital turnover .... _____ times

3. Find for the Industrial Division:

   (a) Invested capital .... $ _____

   (b) Income percentage of revenues .... _____ %

   (c) Rate of return on investment .... _____ %

IV Given for Division 101 of Century Plus Company:

Capital invested in operating assets $3,000,000
Net income 540,000

1. What is the Division's rate of return on investment? .... _____ %

2. If interest is imputed at 16%, what is the amount of residual income? .... $ _____

3. If an available project promises a 17% rate of return on investment, would it tend to be accepted if:

   (a) Rate of return on investment were used to evaluate performance? .... _____
      Why?

      _____

   (b) Residual income were used to evaluate performance? .... _____
      Why?

      _____

V Given for the Dallas Division of State Company:

	Total	Per Unit
Cost of manufacturing 2,000 units of a certain part:		
Variable costs	$120,000	$60
Fixed costs	$ 60,000	$30

Find the total advantage (or disadvantage) to the company if there are at least 2,000 units of idle capacity in the Dallas Division, and if the Austin Division of the same company purchases 2,000 units of this part from an outside supplier at a market price of:

1. $63 per unit .... $ _____

2. $58 per unit .... $ _____

I								
1 b	5 b	9 c	13 c	17 d	21 c	25 c	29 a
2 c	6 b	10 c	14 b	18 c	22 d	26 a	30 a
3 b	7 a	11 a	15 a	19 b	23 c	27 b	31 c
4 b	8 b	12 a	16 d	20 d	24 a	28 b	

Computations:

10 $130 − $120 = $10 disadvantage (c)

11 $120 − $110 = $10 advantage (a)

19 $2,000,000 × 18% = $360,000; $360,000 ÷ 6% = $6 million (b)

20 $32,000 ÷ $800,000 = 4%; 4% × 5 = 20% (d); or $800,000 ÷ 5 = $160,000; $32,000 ÷ $160,000 = 20% (d)

21 2.5 × 6% = 15% (c)

25 $2,000,000 − (14% × $10,000,000) = $600,000 (c)

II   1 goal congruence, 2 goal congruence and managerial effort, 3 the delegation of freedom to make decisions, 4 goal congruence, managerial effort, and segment autonomy, 5 dysfunctional behavior, 6 income divided by invested capital, 7 revenue divided by invested capital, 8 historical cost.

III   Unique Brands, Inc.

1. Maritime Division
   (a) 750,000 ÷ 250,000 = 3 times
   (b) 37,500 ÷ 750,000 = 5%
   (c) 37,500 ÷ 250,000 = 15% (or 3 × 5% = 15%)
2. Farm Division
   (a) 10% × 200,000 = $20,000
   (b) 20,000 ÷ 5% = $400,000
   (c) 400,000 ÷ 200,000 = 2 times
3. Industrial Division
   (a) 450,000 ÷ 4.5 = $100,000
   (b) 13,500 ÷ 450,000 = 3%
   (c) 13,500 ÷ 100,000 = 13.5% (or 4.5 × 3% = 13.5%)

IV   Division 101 of Century Plus Company

1. Net income .... $ 540,000
    Divide by capital invested in operating assets 3,000,000
    Rate of return on investment 18%
2. Net income .... $ 540,000
    Less 16% of $3,000,000 480,000
    Residual income .... $ 60,000
3. (a) No, because the additional project would reduce overall rate of return on investment.
    (b) Yes, because the additional project would increase residual income.

V   Dallas Division of State Company

	(1)	(2)
Variable costs per unit	$60	$60
Outside market price per unit	63	58
Advantage (disadvantage) per unit	($3)	$2
Multiply by number of units	2,000	2,000
Total advantage (disadvantage) to the company	($6,000)	$4,000

(The fixed costs are irrelevant.)

CAPITAL BUDGETING: AN INTRODUCTION

MAIN FOCUS AND OBJECTIVES

Capital budgeting **is the process of arriving at decisions regarding investments in projects covering several years. The leading capital budgeting approach uses:**

- *The concept of time value of money*
- *Procedures for computing discounted cash flows*

We focus on the two main models for selecting and evaluating these long-term investments:

- *Net present value (NPV)*
- *Internal rate of return (IRR)*

Your primary objective is to be able to apply these models to typical capital budgeting situations.

REVIEW OF KEY IDEAS

A. **Capital budgeting** is the process of selecting and evaluating investments in long-term projects.
 1. The conceptually superior approach uses **discounted-cash-flow (DCF)** models because they explicitly and systematically weigh the **time value of money.**
 2. The major assumptions of the DCF models are:
  a. **Predicted cash flows are not uncertain** but are expected to occur as specified (and at the **ends** of the particular years involved).
  b. The **minimum desired rate of return is known** (also called cost of capital, hurdle rate, cutoff rate, target rate, or discount rate).

B. The discounted-cash-flow approach focuses on flows of cash **instead of flows of net income** (revenues minus expenses).

1. The **net-present-value (NPV) model** uses a minimum desired rate of return for discounting cash outflows and inflows to a given point in time so that their net differences may be measured on a common basis.
2. The **internal rate of return (IRR)** is the rate of return (discount rate) that equates the amount invested at a given date with the present value of the expected cash inflows from the investment.

Question: Should depreciation expenses be deducted from the cash inflows when you use these two DCF models?
Answer: No. See below.

3. Because these models are based on inflows and outflows of **cash** and not on the **accrual concepts of revenues and expenses,** no deductions should be made from the operating cash inflows for the periodic allocation of **cost** called **depreciation expense** (which is **not** a cash flow).
    a. In the discounted-cash-flow approaches, the **initial cost** of an asset is typically treated as a **lump-sum outflow** of cash at time zero.
    b. Therefore, to also deduct periodic depreciation from periodic cash inflows would be a **double-counting** of this cost.
4. Each DCF model has a **different decision rule:**
    a. If the **internal rate of return** equals or exceeds the minimum desired rate of return, accept the project; if not, reject the project.
    b. If the **net present value** is zero or positive, accept the project; if not, reject the project.

C. There is always some **uncertainty** that cash-flow predictions will actually be realized.
    1. Ways to recognize this risk for riskier projects:
        a. Use higher discount rates.
        b. Reduce expected lives.
        c. Predict lower cash inflows and higher cash outflows.
    2. **Sensitivity analysis** also helps recognize risk:
        a. Make and compare three separate predictions for a given project: **pessimistic, expected,** and **optimistic.**
        b. Determine the amount of deviation from expected values that would cause a change in the decision.
        c. By providing an immediate financial measure of the possible errors in forecasting, sensitivity analysis helps managers to concentrate attention on the most sensitive decision factors in a given case.

D. The **same net-present-value difference** between two alternative projects is obtainable by either of two approaches for discounting cash flows to a common present date.

See textbook Exhibit 11-4

1. **The total project approach:**
    a. Calculate the **net present value of the cash flows** of each of the two projects.
    b. Find the **difference between these net present values.**
2. **The incremental approach:**
    a. For each year, find the **difference between the cash flows** of each of the two projects.
    b. Calculate the **net present value of these differences.**

E. Summary of typical matters to be considered in making cash-flow analyses:
1. **Current disposal values** of old assets are most conveniently handled by **offsetting** them against the gross cash outlays for new assets at time zero.
2. All initial investments (including receivables, inventories, intangibles) are typically regarded as cash outflows at time zero, and their terminal disposal values (if any) are treated as cash inflows at the end of the project's useful life.
3. Errors in forecasting future disposal values are usually **not crucial** because the combination of relatively small disposal values and long time periods tends to produce rather small present values.
4. Depreciation and book values are **ignored** because they are **cost allocations, not cash flows.**
5. In the relevant-cost analysis of factory overhead, the only pertinent cost is the overhead that will **differ among alternatives.**
6. **Income taxes and inflation do affect cash flows,** but they are postponed for consideration until the next chapter.
7. When cash-flow analysis is applied to **two mutually exclusive projects,** the one that shows the **larger net present value** should be undertaken.
8. When alternative projects being considered have unequal lives, comparisons should be made over either the useful life of the longer project or the useful life of the shorter project.

F. Discounted-cash-flow approaches are recommended for reaching capital-budgeting decisions, but several **conceptually inferior techniques or models** are recognized here because they are used in many businesses:
1. The **emergency-persuasion method** uses no formal planning but seems to be based mainly on urgency caused by procrastination and neglect (not recommended).
2. The **payback, payout,** or **payoff model** measures the estimated number of years before cash inflows return the initial cash investment.
    a. If cash flows are **uniform,** the initial cash investment is divided by the annual cash inflow; if cash flows are **not uniform,** a **cumulative approach** is used.

> **This method ignores the profitability of investments, but it is popular.**

3. The **accounting-rate-of-return model** is also called the accounting model, the financial-statement model, the book-value model, the rate-of-return-on-assets model, and the approximate-rate-of-return model.
    a. The predicted amount of future average annual net income, or increase therein, is divided by the initial (sometimes average) amount of the required investment, or increase therein.

> **This model is widely used, but it ignores the time value of money.**

     b. However, because this approach aims at profit measurement by **conventional accrual accounting methods,** it usually facilitates a **follow-up** or **postaudit** of a capital-budgeting decision.

G. Despite the conceptual advantages of DCF models, many managers are reluctant to adopt them because of the wide usage of the accrual accounting model for evaluating performance.

     1. To avoid such a conflict, managers often use the accrual accounting model for capital-budgeting purposes.

     2. However, it is feasible in some instances to use the DCF model for decisions and also for a performance evaluation audit on an individual project basis.

     3. Another approach is to use **both** models at the decision point and then compare performance on the accrual accounting basis.

PRACTICE TEST QUESTIONS AND PROBLEMS WITH SOLUTIONS

I For each of the following multiple-choice and true-false statements, select the most appropriate answer and enter its identification letter in the space provided:

___ 1. The DCF model usually assumes: (a) certain cash flows, (b) a minimum desired rate of return, (c) both of these, (d) neither of these.

___ 2. Discounted cash flows and the time value of money are involved in: (a) the net-present-value method, (b) the internal rate of return method, (c) both of these, (d) neither of these.

___ 3. The internal rate of return is the discount rate that produces a zero NPV: (a) true, (b) false.

___ 4. A project has a positive NPV using a 15% discount rate. Its IRR would be: (a) 15%, (b) greater than 15%, (c) less than 15%.

___ 5. If a project has a negative NPV, the IRR is higher than the discount rate used to compute NPV: (a) true, (b) false.

___ 6. A negative NPV on a project would indicate a lower IRR than the discount rate used to compute NPV: (a) true, (b) false.

___ 7. The present value of $50,000 due five years from now would be lowest if computed at a discount rate of: (a) 6%, (b) 12%, (c) zero %.

___ 8. If a project has a positive NPV, the positive NPV measures the prospective profit on the project: (a) true, (b) false.

___ 9. Two projects promise the same amounts and timing of cash inflows, but Project A requires an immediate cash outflow of $100,000 while Project B requires a $50,000 cash outflow now and a $54,000 cash outflow one year from now. The project with the larger NPV, using a 10% discount rate is: (a) A, (b) B.

___ 10. Pom Co. is considering the purchase of a special-purpose machine for $53,000. The machine has a twelve-year estimated life, a $5,000 residual value after twelve years, and expected cash operating savings of $11,000 per year. Compute the payback period: (a) 4.4 years, (b) 7.6 years, (c) 4.8 years, (d) 6.9 years.

___ 11. See the preceding test item. Compute the accounting rate of return on the initial investment: (a) 20.8%, (b) 22.9%, (c) 14.6%, (d) 13.2%.

___ 12. See the Pom Co. data in item 10 above. Present-value tables at 16% show 0.168 and 5.197, respectively, for present values of $1 and an annuity of $1. Compute

NPV: (a) $5,007, (b) $9,167, (c) $4,167, (d) none of these.

_____ 13. The use of the discounted-cash-flow approach requires that periodic depreciation expense be: (a) added to cash flows, (b) deducted from cash flows, (c) neither of these.

_____ 14. Discounted-cash-flow tables and techniques are designed to provide for recovery of principal or investment: (a) true, (b) false.

_____ 15. Ways to recognize the risk of uncertainty include: (a) using sensitivity analysis, (b) making lower predictions of cash inflows, (c) both of these, (d) neither of these.

_____ 16. Jan Co. is considering the purchase of equipment for $10,000. The company anticipates annual cash savings of $4,000 for four years with no residual value. Compute NPV at a 10% discount rate. A table shows the discount factor to be 3.170. Compute NPV: (a) $2,680, (b) $12,680, (c) $6,000, (d) none of these.

_____ 17. See the preceding test item. Compute the annual cash flow at the point of indifference, the point where the net present value would be zero: (a) $3,170, (b) $10,317, (c) $3,155, (d) none of these.

_____ 18. Generally, in cash-flow analysis, we should ignore book value: (a) true, (b) false.

_____ 19. The most convenient way to handle disposal values of old assets when making a discounted cash-flow analysis is to: (a) add them to the required investment in the project, (b) treat them as cash outflows, (c) treat them as cash inflows, (d) offset them against gross cash outlays for new assets.

_____ 20. Usually, errors in forecasting future disposal values of assets are: (a) crucial, (b) not crucial.

_____ 21. The profitability of an investment is ignored by: (a) the accounting-rate-of-return model, (b) the payback model, (c) both of these, (d) neither of these.

_____ 22. The time value of money is ignored by the accounting-rate-of-return model: (a) true, (b) false.

_____ 23. A project requires an immediate investment of $50,000 cash, and it promises cash returns at the end of each year as follows: first year $10,000, second year $12,000, third year $13,000, fourth year $15,000, fifth year $20,000, and sixth (and final) year $30,000. The payback period in years is: (a) two, (b) three, (c) four, (d) five, (e) some other number.

_____ 24. A project requires an immediate investment of $60,000 in some new equipment with an estimated useful life of ten years and no residual value. If predicted annual savings of cash operating expenses are $15,000, what is the accounting rate of return based on the initial investment? Use straight-line depreciation and ignore income taxes: (a) 25%, (b) 20%, (c) 15%, (d) 10%, (e) some other rate.

_____ 25. A follow-up or postaudit of a capital-budgeting decision is facilitated by the use of: (a) the net-present-value method, (b) the accounting-rate-of-return model, (c) both of these, (d) neither of these.

_____ 26. The adoption of the discounted-cash-flow approach to capital-budgeting decisions is: (a) helped by the continued use of conventional accrual accounting methods, (b) hindered by the continued use of conventional accrual accounting methods.

II Complete each of the following statements:

1. A proposed project should be accepted if the internal rate of return is _____ than the _____ _____ .

2. If expected annual cash flows are uniform, the payback period can be computed by dividing

_____

by _____ .

III Given for Fast-Flow Fire Hose Co.:

Minimum desired rate of return	10%
Present value of $1 due 13 years from now, using a 10% effective interest rate	$0.29
Present value of $1 per year due at the end of each of 13 years from now, using a 10% effective interest rate	$7.10
Initial cost of a special-purpose machine	$40,000
Predicted useful life	13 yrs.
Predicted residual value at end of useful life	$ 5,000
Predicted annual savings in cash operating expenses (increase in annual cash operating income)	$ 6,000

Compute the following, ignoring income tax effects:

Present value of predicted residual value:

_____ $ _____

Present value of predicted cash inflows from annual savings in cash operating expenses:

_____ $ _____

Total present value of expected cash inflows .... $ _____

Less the initial cost of the machine .... $ _____

Net present value of the project .... $ _____

IV Given for Newman Pneumatic Tube Company:

Initial cost of a special-purpose machine	$90,000
Predicted useful life (no terminal scrap value)	15 yrs.
Predicted annual savings in cash operating expenses	$15,000
Present value of an annuity of $1 for 15 years:	
Using a 14% effective interest rate	$ 6.142
Using a 16% effective interest rate	$ 5.575

Find the internal rate of return to the nearest tenth of a percent, ignoring income tax effects:

Payback period: $ _____ divided by $ _____ = _____ yrs.

Rate of Return	Present-Value Factors	
14%	_____	_____
True rate		_____
16%	_____	
Differences	_____	_____

Computations: _____

_____

_____

_____

Internal rate of return .... _____ %

V Given for Capitol Dome Flag Company:

Initial cost of proposed new equipment $60,000
Predicted useful life .... 10 yrs.
Predicted residual value at end of useful life .... none
Predicted savings per year in cash operating expenses $15,000

Compute each of the following, ignoring income tax effects:

1. Payback period: _____

   _____ _____ yrs.

2. Depreciation expense per year by straight-line method: _____

   _____ $ _____

3. Predicted increase in future annual net income: _____

   _____ $ _____

4. Accounting rate of return based on initial investment: _____

   _____ _____ %

CHAPTER 11 SOLUTIONS TO PRACTICE TEST QUESTIONS AND PROBLEMS

I

1 c	5 b	9 b	13 c	17 c	21 b	25 b
2 c	6 a	10 c	14 a	18 a	22 a	26 b
3 a	7 b	11 d	15 c	19 d	23 c	
4 b	8 b	12 a	16 a	20 b	24 c	

Computations:

10 53,000 ÷ 11,000 = 4.8 years (c)

11 Depreciation is (53,000 − 5,000) ÷ 12 = $4,000 per year;
   (11,000 − 4,000) ÷ 53,000 = 7,000 ÷ 53,000 = 13.2% (d)

12 (5,000 × .168) + (11,000 × 5.197) = 840 + 57,167 = 58,007;
   58,007 − 53,000 = $5,007 (a)

16 (4,000 × 3.170) − 10,000 = 12,680 − 10,000 = $2,680 (a)

17 $0 = 3.170x - 10,000$; $3.170x = 10,000$;
   $x = 10,000 ÷ 3.170 = \$3,155$ (c)

23 10,000 + 12,000 + 13,000 + 15,000 = 50,000. Therefore payback period is four years (c)

24 Depreciation is 60,000 ÷ 10 = $6,000 per year;
   (15,000 − 6,000) ÷ 60,000 = 9,000 ÷ 60,000 = 15% (c)

II   1 greater, the minimum desired rate of return, 2 the initial cash investment, the annual cash inflow.

III   Fast-Flow Fire Hose Co.

Present value of predicted residual value is $5,000 × 0.29	$ 1,450
·Present value of predicted cash inflows from annual savings in cash operating expenses is $6,000 × 7.10	42,600
Present value of total expected cash inflows	$44,050
Less the initial cost of the machine	40,000
Net present value of the project	$ 4,050

IV   Newman Pneumatic Tube Company

Payback period is $90,000 divided by $15,000 .... 6yrs.

Rate of return	Present-Value Factors	
14%	6.142	6.142
True rate		6.000
16%	5.575	—
2% Differences	.567	.142

Computations: 14% + 2% (.142 ÷ .567)
   = 14% + 2% (.25)
   = 14% + .5%
   = 14.5%, the internal rate of return

V   Capitol Dome Flag Company

1. Payback period: $60,000 ÷ $15,000 .... 4 yrs.
2. Depreciation expense per year: $60,000 ÷ 10 yrs. $6,000
3. Predicted increase in future annual net income: $15,000 − $6,000 .... $9,000
4. Accounting rate of return based on initial investment: $9,000 ÷ $60,000 .... 15%

Chapter **12**

CAPITAL BUDGETING:
TAXES AND INFLATION

MAIN FOCUS AND OBJECTIVES

To lessen a steep learning slope in the preceding chapter, we ignored *income tax effects* on capital budgeting decisions. This chapter deals with those effects, principally the effects of depreciation. The central idea is:

- *Depreciation produces cash savings in income taxes*

Your primary objective is to be able to make a capital budgeting analysis that includes *all* income tax effects. An important secondary objective is to include in your analysis the:

- *Effects of price inflation*

REVIEW OF KEY IDEAS

A. Both the **amount** and **timing** of cash flows are directly affected by income taxation.
   1. Depreciation is a **noncash expense** used in computing periodic net income.

> **See textbook Exhibit 12-1**

     a. Because depreciation expense is subtracted in arriving at the amount of periodic net income but is not a periodic cash disbursement, it may be **added back** to the net income figure to arrive at current net cash inflow from all revenue-producing operations.
     b. Although depreciation itself is not a cash inflow, the deductibility of depreciation from revenues in determining net income subject to taxes will reduce income tax payments and thus serves as an important **tax shield.**
   2. The tax savings from depreciation have a present value.

See textbook Exhibit 12-2

     a. See **Method Two** of this exhibit, and be sure you understand it.

3. The present value of the tax savings from depreciation is increased by **accelerated depreciation:**

     a. The most recently permitted method in the United States is the **Accelerated Cost Recovery System (ACRS)** (See textbook Exhibits 12-3 and 12-4).

     b. This method is required in the U.S. for most depreciable assets placed in service since 1980.

     c. In comparison with the straight-line depreciation, note the **enhancement of present values** of income tax savings that can be provided by the ACRS method.

See textbook Exhibit 12-5

B. Pause at this point to make sure that you clearly understand the central idea of this chapter and how to apply it.

> **Question: What are the key textbook illustrations that are most helpful for this purpose?**
> **Answer: See below.**

1. **Exhibit 12-2** computes net present value in a straight-line depreciation situation.

2. The first **Summary Problem for Your Review** uses ACRS plus a terminal value at the end of the project's life.

C. Discounted-cash-flow models should be adjusted for the effects of price inflation (the decline in the general purchasing power of money).

1. The discount rate should be increased to include an element representing the rate of inflation.

2. The expected after-tax cash operating inflows should be adjusted upward by this same rate.

3. See textbook **Exhibit 12-7,** which contrasts a correct analysis with an incorrect analysis.

     a. The key is **consistency** in using an inflation element in both the discount rate and the predicted operating cash flows.

> **Question: Why does the correct analysis exclude an inflation adjustment for the income tax savings from depreciation?**
> **Answer: The U.S. income tax law requires depreciation to be based on cost in terms of the dollars of time zero.**

PRACTICE TEST QUESTIONS AND PROBLEMS WITH SOLUTIONS

I For each of the following multiple-choice and true-false statements, select the most appropriate answer and enter its identification letter in the space provided:

___ 1. Examples of tax shields include: (a) depreciation of equipment, (b) salaries of employees, (c) both depreciation and salaries, (d) neither depreciation nor salaries.

___ 2. Toc Co. has an income tax rate of 35% and depreciation expense of $100,000. The value of the tax savings from depreciation is: (a) $35,000, (b) $65,000, (c) $100,000, (d) none.

___ 3. See the preceding test item. The after-tax effect of the depreciation expense on net income is a decrease of: (a), (b), (c), (d).

___ 4. See item 2 above. The current net cash inflow from revenue-producing operations is net income plus: (a), (b), (c), (d).

___ 5. Book values and depreciation can, by themselves, be relevant to: (a) the decision model, (b) the prediction method, (c) both the decision model and the prediction method, (d) neither the decision model nor the prediction method.

___ 6. Assume two expenses of a business: cash advertising $20,000 and depreciation $20,000. If the income tax rate is 30%, the after-tax effects on cash would be an outflow $14,000 for advertising and an inflow $6,000 for depreciation: (a) true, (b) false.

___ 7. Given for a certain company: sales $200,000, depreciation expense $20,000, other expenses $150,000, income tax rate 40%. Compute net income: (a) $30,000, (b) $18,000, (c) $12,000, (d) $20,000, (e) some other amount.

___ 8. See the preceding test item. Compute the after-tax effect of operations on cash: (a) $32,000, (b) $40,000, (c) $50,000, (d) $38,000, (e) some other amount.

___ 9. See item 7 above. Compute the after-tax effect of depreciation on cash: (a) $8,000, (b) $12,000, (c) $20,000, (d) $30,000, (e) some other amount.

___ 10. Given for a new machine purchased by a company: cost $60,000, expected useful life 5 years, expected terminal disposal value $15,000. Compute the depreciation for the **second** year by the ACRS method: (a) $9,900, (b) $9,000, (c) $12,600, (d) $14,400, (e) some other amount.

___ 11. See the preceding test item. Compute the depreciation for the **second** year by the straight-line method: (a) $12,000, (b) $15,000, (c) $9,000, (d) none of these.

___ 12. See items 10 and 11 above. If the income tax rate is 60%, the tax-saving effect of the ACRS method over the straight-line method for the **second** year would be: (a) $3,240, (b) $1,680, (c) $4,200, (d) none of these.

___ 13. Non Co. sold for $44,000 cash an old piece of equipment. It was purchased 8 years ago for $130,000 and was being depreciated on a straight-line basis over a useful life of 10 years with an expected terminal scrap value of $10,000. What was the gain or loss on the sale before income taxes? (a) $20,000 gain, (b) $18,000 loss, (c) $10,000 gain, (d) some other gain or loss.

___ 14. See the preceding test item. Compute the after-tax cash increase from the sale transaction only, assuming a 40% income tax rate: (a) $40,000, (b) $17,600, (c) $26,400, (d) some other amount.

___ 15. The expected future cash flows caused by income tax savings from depreciation should be adjusted by the rate of inflation before being discounted to the present: (a) true, (b) false.

___ 16. To compensate for the effects of inflation, one should adjust the discounted-cash-flow model by increasing both the discount rate and the cash operating inflows: (a) true, (b) false.

II Given for Electric Deflector Corporation's 19X5 operations:

Sales	$900,000
Straight-line depreciation expense	40,000
Other operating expenses, including cost of goods sold	700,000
Income tax rate	40%

1. Compute net income

   Sales .... $ 900,000

   Less _____   _____

   _____   _____

   _____   _____

   _____   _____

   Net income _____ $ _____

2. Compute the after-tax effect of depreciation on net income:

   Depreciation .... $ 40,000

   Less _____   _____

   After-tax effect of depreciation on net income _____ $ _____

3. Compute the annual value of the income tax savings from depreciation:

   Depreciation .... $ 40,000

   Multiply by _____   _____

   Annual value of the income tax savings from depreciation .... $ _____

4. Compute the after-tax net cash inflow from operations:

   Sales .... $ 900,000

   Less _____   _____

   _____   _____

   After-tax net cash inflow from operations .... $ _____

III Abraham Co. sold for $90,000 cash some of its old manufacturing machinery. This machinery was purchased ten years ago for $280,000. It was being depreciated on a straight-line basis over a useful life of twelve years with an estimated terminal salvage value of $40,000.

1. Compute the after-tax cash effect of the sale transaction only, assuming a 45% income tax rate.

2. Assume the same facts except that the machinery was purchased eight years ago. Compute the after-tax cash effect of the sale transaction only.

IV Fellini Company has just purchased a special piece of manufacturing equipment for $450,000. It is estimated to have a useful life of five years and a terminal scrap value of $30,000. Compute the following:

1. Depreciation for the first year:
   (a) Straight-line method .... $ _____
   (b) ACRS .... $ _____

2. Depreciation for the second year by ACRS .... $ _____

3. Income tax saving effect of ACRS compared with the straight-line

   method for the second year, assuming a 60% income tax rate .... $ _____

V Using the data below for Expeditious Express Co., compute net present value:

Purchase price of special equipment	$80,000
Predicted useful life	8 yrs
Predicted annual savings in cash operating costs	$25,000
Predicted residual value (terminal scrap value)	none
Depreciation method: straight-line	
Minimum desired **after-tax** rate of return	12%
Income tax rate	30%
Present value of annuity of $1 for eight years at 12% (rounded)	$5.00

VI Mantis Company's discount rate of 24% for capital budgeting includes an 8% inflation element. Assume a 40% income tax rate and compute the present value of:

1. A $60,000 pretax cash operating inflow one year from now.

2. The income tax savings of a $20,000 depreciation expense one year from now.

CHAPTER 12 SOLUTIONS TO PRACTICE TEST QUESTIONS AND PROBLEMS

I

1 c	5 b	9 a	13 c
2 a	6 a	10 d	14 a
3 b	7 b	11 c	15 b
4 c	8 d	12 a	16 a

Computations:

2 $35\% \times 100,000 = \$35,000$ (a)

3 $100,000 - 35,000 = \$65,000$ (b)

6 $70\% \times 20,000 = \$14,000$; $30\% \times 20,000 = \$6,000$ (a)

7 $200,000 - 20,000 - 150,000 = 30,000$; $30,000 \times 40\% = 12,000$;
$30,000 - 12,000 = \$18,000$ (b)

8 $18,000 + 20,000 = \$38,000$ (d); or $200,000 - 150,000 - 12,000 = \$38,000$; or
$(200,000 - 150,000) \times 60\% = 30,000$; $20,000 \times 40\% = 8,000$; $30,000 + 8,000 = \$38,000$

9 $20,000 \times 40\% = 8,000$ (a)

10 $24\% \times 60,000 = \$14,400$ (d)

11 $60,000 - 15,000 = 45,000$; $45,000 \div 5 = \$9,000$ straight-line depreciation (c)

12 $60\% (14,400 - 9,000) = 60\% \times 5,400 - 3,240$ (a)

13 Annual depreciation: $(\$130,000 - \$10,000) \div 10 = \$12,000$; net book value when sold:
$\$130,000 - 8(\$12,000) = \$34,000$; gain on sale: $\$44,000 - \$34,000 = \$10,000$ (c)

14 Tax on gain: $40\% \times \$10,000 = \$4,000$; after-tax cash: $\$44,000 - \$4,000 = \$40,000$ (a)

II   Electric Deflector Corporation

1. Sales		$900,000
Less:		
Depreciation expense	$ 40,000	
Other operating expenses	700,000	740,000
Income before income taxes		$160,000
Less income taxes at 40%		64,000
Net income		$ 96,000
2. Depreciation		$ 40,000
Less tax reduction effect at 40%		16,000
After-tax effect of depreciation on net income, a decrease		$ 24,000
3. Depreciation		$ 40,000
Multiply by income tax rate		40%
Annual value of income tax savings from depreciation		$ 16,000
4. Sales		$900,000
Less:		
Other operating expenses	$700,000	
Income taxes, from (1) above	64,000	764,000
After-tax net cash inflow from operations		$136,000
Alternative computational methods for (4):		
(a) Net income, from (1) above		$ 96,000
Add back depreciation		40,000
After-tax net cash inflow from operations		$136,000

(b) Sales		$900,000
Less other operating expenses		700,000
Cash inflows from operations before taxes and the depreciation effect		$200,000
Less applicable income tax outflow at 40%		80,000
After-tax effect of cash inflow from operations before the depreciation effect		$120,000
Add annual value of tax savings from depreciation: 40% of $40,000		16,000
After-tax net cash inflow from operations		$136,000

III   Abraham Co.

	1.	2.
Depreciation per year: ($280,000 − $40,000) ÷ 12	$ 20,000	$ 20,000
Multiply by age when sold	× 10	× 8
Accumulated depreciation	$200,000	$160,000
Original cost	280,000	280,000
Net book value when sold	$ 80,000	$120,000
Sold for cash	90,000(a)	90,000(a)
Gain on sale	$ 10,000	
Loss on sale		$ 30,000
Tax: $10,000 × 45%	$ 4,500(b)	
Tax saving: $30,000 × 45%		$ 13,500(c)
After-tax effect on sale:		
(a) minus (b)	$ 85,500	
(a) plus (c)		$103,500

IV   Fellini Company

1. (a) ($450,000 − $30,000) ÷ 5 = $84,000
   (b) 40% ($450,000) = $180,000
2. 24% ($450,000) = $108,000
3. ($108,000 − $84,000)(60%) = $14,400

V   Expeditious Express Co.

Annual savings in cash operating costs		$ 25,000
Less income taxes at 30%		7,500
After-tax effect of expected annual cash savings in operating costs		$ 17,500
Annual depreciation: $80,000 ÷ 8	$10,000	
Multiply by income tax rate	30%	
Value of expected annual income tax savings from depreciation		3,000
Total expected annual increase in after-tax net cash inflow		$ 20,500
Multiply by present value of annuity of $1 at 12% for 8 years		5
Total present value of expected annual increase in after-tax net cash inflow		$102,500
Less cost of the investment		80,000
Net present value of the investment		$ 22,500

VI Mantis Company

Using a 24% discount rate, the present value of $1 to be received one year from now is $.8065.
1. $60,000 − 40\%(\$60,000) = \$36,000$; $\$36,000 \times 1.08 \times .8065 = \$31,357$
2. $\$20,000 \times 40\% \times .8065 = \$6,452$

Chapter 13

JOB-COSTING SYSTEMS AND OVERHEAD APPLICATION

MAIN FOCUS AND OBJECTIVES

This chapter examines manufacturing costs, particularly the job-costing system and the application of factory overhead costs to products. Your first main objective is to clearly understand:

- *The typical transactions involving manufacturing costs*
- *The matching flows of these costs through ledger accounts*

The other main objectives are to learn:

- *how to use predetermined rates in applying factory overhead cost to products*

REVIEW OF KEY IDEAS

A. Two product costing systems are widely used:
1. **Job-order costing** is suitable for the manufacture of custom-made products or other products that are readily identified by individual units or batches, each of which receives varying degrees of attention and skill, for example: furniture, machinery, highway bridges, and drilling platforms for off-shore oil exploration.
2. In contrast, **process costing** is appropriate for the mass production of uniform units, which usually flow continuously through a series of standard production steps called operations or processes, for example: textiles, chemicals, petroleum products, cement, bricks, newsprint, ice cream, and breakfast foods.

B. Job-order costing essentially involves **cost application,** which is the identification of accumulated costs with specific jobs or orders of products.

> See textbook Exhibit 13-1

1. The central form is this **job-cost sheet:**
   a. Material requisitions are used to apply **direct-material costs.**
   b. Time tickets are used to apply **direct-labor costs.**
   c. Predetermined rates are used to apply **factory-overhead costs.**
2. The typical transactions for manufacturing activities are described:

> **See textbook Exhibit 13-2**

   a. Note carefully the **formal journal entries** and the accompanying detailed transaction analyses in the textbook.
   b. Observe the **cost flows** through the general ledger accounts in Exhibit 13-2.

3. **Question: Why is factory overhead applied by predetermined rates?**

Answer:

   a. Many factory costs are **indirect** manufacturing costs and thus cannot be identified with specific jobs.
   b. Therefore the amount of factory overhead cost applicable to specific jobs must be **estimated** by using rates based upon total direct labor cost, total direct labor-hours, total machine-hours, or some other base common to all jobs worked on.

4. **Question: What are these predetermined rates and how are they used?**

Answer:

   a. The rates are computed **on an annual basis** by dividing **budgeted** factory overhead by the **budgeted** rate base (that is, the budgeted cost allocation base, such as machine-hours or direct-labor cost).
   b. Applied overhead is the predetermined rate times the **actual** rate base.
   c. The excess of the applied overhead over the actual overhead incurred is called **overapplied overhead or overabsorbed overhead.**
   d. If the actual amount of overhead incurred exceeds the applied amount, the difference is called **underapplied or underabsorbed.**

5. **Question: Why aren't actual overhead cost rates calculated at the end of the year by using actual overhead costs incurred and actual overhead application bases?**

Answer:

   a. The resulting cost information, although relatively **more accurate,** would usually not be available **on a timely basis** for product pricing, inventory valuation, and income measurement.

     b. Therefore many companies use **normalized overhead rates** that are based upon **budgeted** amounts of factory-overhead costs and rate bases, as described above in 4.

     c. Such **predetermined** factory-overhead rates are typically used on an **annualized basis rather than a monthly basis** in order to overcome cost distortions due to month-to-month fluctuations in production volume and overhead costs.

     d. Thus we can obtain a **more realistic measure** of product costs for reporting inventories and for pricing product sales.

C.

> **Question: How is the amount of underapplied or overapplied overhead disposed of?**

> **See textbook Exhibit 13-3**

1. This is done only **at the end of the year.**
2. If there is a **relatively large** difference, it may be **prorated.**
   a. This means that the amount is allocated to the three balances that were affected by the use of predetermined overhead rates: work-in-process inventory, finished-goods inventory, and cost of goods sold.
   b. This method tends to adjust applied costs to an actual basis and is therefore conceptually appealing if the difference is due to forecasting errors.
3. However, if the underapplied or overapplied amount is **relatively small,** as it typically is, it is **not prorated.**
   a. This means that it is simply written off directly to cost of goods sold (an addition if factory overhead is underapplied, a subtraction if overapplied).
   b. The theoretical justification for such treatment is that typically there is underapplied overhead and it is due mostly to **inefficiencies** or to the **underutilization of available facilities** (which would not be appropriate costs of the inventory assets).

D. Due to the existence of fixed costs, overhead application is the most troublesome aspect of product costing.
1. Most companies combine all overhead costs in computing a **single overhead application rate,** thus making no distinction between variable- and fixed-cost behavior.
2. However, some companies use **separate rates for variable and fixed overhead** for both product costing and management control purposes.

E. The cost system we are describing is sometimes called an **actual cost system.**
1. However, it is more accurately called a **normal cost system** because the factory overhead included in product costs is not the actual amount incurred but is the amount applied by means of predetermined overhead rates.
2. Typically, the normal system is used to cost products during the year, and the year-end procedures described above in C are used to convert total results to an approximate actual-cost basis.

F. The job costing approach described for manufacturing companies can also be used for nonprofit organizations.
1. Instead of costs being allocated to **tangible jobs,** they may be allocated to **programs,** which are identifiable groups of activities that produce **intangible services.**
2. However, in nonprofit organizations, it is usually harder to measure **benefits** against

these costs because **market prices** are rarely available to measure the values of the benefits.

G. A popular hybrid costing system is called **operation costing, hybrid costing,** or **specification costing.**
  1. This method is a blend of ideas from the systems of job-order costing and process costing.
  2. An **operation** is defined as a standardized method or technique.
    a. Examples include milling, cleaning, and grinding.
    b. Such procedures are applied in like manner to batches of **different products.**
  3. **Direct material costs** are identified with specific product batches (the job-cost idea).
  4. **Conversion costs** (direct labor and factory overhead) are identified with the particular operation (the process-cost idea):
    a. An average conversion cost per unit is applied to the units passing through each operation.
    b. An average material cost per unit is applied to the units in a batch, which passes through one or more operations.

H. To gain a useful perspective of the important relationships among the manufacturing inventories reported in the **balance sheet** and the cost of goods sold and underapplied overhead reported in the **income statement:**

> See textbook Exhibit 13-4

PRACTICE TEST QUESTIONS AND PROBLEMS WITH SOLUTIONS

I For each of the following multiple-choice and true-false statements, select the most appropriate answer and enter its identification letter in the space provided:

_____ 1. In a job-order cost system, indirect factory labor wages paid should be debited to: (a) Labor in Process, (b) Factory Department Overhead Control, (c) Work in Process, (d) none of these.

_____ 2. In a job-order cost system, the purchase of direct materials should be debited to: (a) Material Purchases, (b) Work in Process, (c) Direct Material Inventory, (d) none of these.

_____ 3. In a job-order cost system, factory overhead applied should be debited to: (a) Work in Process, (b) Factory Department Overhead Control, (c) Cost of Goods Sold, (d) none of these.

_____ 4. In a job-order cost system, the issuance of direct materials to production should be credited to: (a) Direct Materials Used, (b) Work in Process, (c) Accounts Payable, (d) none of these.

_____ 5. Examples of products for which a job-order costing system would probably be suitable include: (a) machinery, (b) petroleum, (c) both of these, (d) neither of these.

_____ 6. Examples of products for which a process cost system would probably be suitable include: (a) bricks, (b) textiles, (c) both of these, (d) neither of these.

_____ 7. In an operation costing system, direct material costs are identified with specific product batches, and conversion costs are identified with specific jobs: (a) true, (b) false.

_____ 8. Compared with the use of actual factory overhead rates, the use of predetermined rates would provide the accumulation of cost data that are: (a) more accurate and more timely, (b) less accurate but more timely, (c) less accurate and less timely, (d) more accurate but less timely.

___ 9. Most companies charge overhead costs to products on the basis of: (a) actual overhead rates, (b) normalized overhead rates.

___ 10. When predetermined rates are used for applying factory overhead to production, they should usually be computed on a monthly or quarterly basis: (a) true, (b) false.

___ 11. A manufacturing company budgeted for 19X3 40,000 total direct labor-hours and $220,000 of factory overhead costs. However, the actual 19X3 amounts were 44,000 hours and $240,000 cost, respectively. Compute the proper rate for applying overhead to production: (a) $5.00, (b) $5.45, (c) $5.50, (d) $6.00, (e) some other rate.

___ 12. See the preceding test item. The applied overhead should be: (a) $220,000, (b) $240,000, (c) $242,000, (d) $264,000, (e) some other amount.

___ 13. See item 11 above. Factory overhead in 19X3 was (a) $2,000 overapplied, (b) $2,000 underapplied, (c) $20,000 overapplied, (d) $20,000 underapplied, (e) some other amount overapplied or underapplied.

___ 14. A company reported for 19X4 sales of $790,000, cost of goods sold $515,000 (including $190,000 of applied overhead), and overapplied overhead amounting to $10,000. The actual factory overhead incurred was: (a) $190,000, (b) $200,000, (c) $180,000, (d) some other amount.

___ 15. See the preceding test item. If end-of-year overhead differences were not prorated, the gross profit was: (a) $285,000, (b) $265,000, (c) $275,000, (d) some other amount.

___ 16. Underapplied factory overhead is the excess of incurred overhead over the amount of: (a) budgeted factory overhead, (b) actual factory overhead, (c) applied factory overhead, (d) estimated factory overhead.

___ 17. The typical end-of-year treatment of underapplied or overapplied factory overhead is to assign all of it to: (a) work in process and finished goods, (b) cost of goods sold, (c) both of these, (d) neither of these.

___ 18. Because underapplied overhead is caused largely by inefficiencies or by the under-utilization of available facilities, the end-of-year treatment that would be justified is: (a) a lump-sum write-off to cost of goods sold, (b) a proration over finished goods inventory, work-in-process inventory, and cost of goods sold.

___ 19. Actual direct-labor costs incurred are included in product costs in: (a) an actual cost system, (b) a normal cost system, (c) both of these, (d) neither of these.

___ 20. A job-costing approach is ordinarily not appropriate for use in nonprofit organizations that produce intangible services: (a) true, (b) false.

II Complete each of the following statements:

1. There should be a strong correlation between factory-overhead cost incurred and the _____ _____ .

2. Costs of materials used in production are carried through three inventory accounts:

(a) _____

(b) _____

(c) _____

3. Predetermined factory-overhead rates can be computed by dividing _____ _____ cost by _____ _____ .

4. Applied factory-overhead cost is determined by multiplying the _____ by the _____ .

5. At the end of the year, if the underapplied or overapplied factory-overhead cost is to be treated in a theoretically correct and precise manner, it should be prorated over three accounts:

(a) _____

(b) _____

(c) _____

III Apogee Products Company presents the following data for 19X5:

Beginning inventories:

Direct material	$ 40,000
Work in process	32,000
Finished goods	36,000

Transactions for the year:

Direct-material purchases on account	$160,000
Direct labor incurred	190,000
Factory overhead incurred	153,000
Factory overhead applied	148,000
Direct materials used	150,000
Work in process completed	498,000
Normal cost of goods sold	496,000
Sales on account	750,000

Compute the following, assuming that the year-end overhead differences are not prorated:

1. Ending inventories:

   (a) Direct material .... $ _____

   (b) Work in process .... $ _____

   (c) Finished goods .... $ _____

2. Adjusted cost of goods sold .... $ _____

3. Gross profit on sales .... $ _____

IV Given for Ceiling Fans, Inc.:

Budgeted factory-overhead cost	$80,000
Budgeted machine-hours	50,000 hrs.
Actual factory-overhead cost incurred	$85,000
Actual machine-hours used	55,000 hrs.

1. Compute:

   (a) Predetermined overhead rate: $ _____

   (b) Applied factory-overhead cost: $ _____

   (c) Amount of overhead underapplied or overapplied: $ _____

2. Prepare the journal entry to write off the amount in (c) at year-end (without proration):

_____

_____

V Given for Special Appurtenances Company:

Selling and administrative expenses	$210,000
Sales	800,000
Cost of goods sold at normal cost	530,000
Overapplied factory overhead	12,000

Prepare the income statement:

_____ $ _____

_____   _____

_____   _____

_____   _____

_____   _____

_____   _____

_____   _____

I	1 b	5 a	9 b	13 a	17 b
	2 c	6 c	10 b	14 c	18 a
	3 a	7 b	11 c	15 a	19 c
	4 d	8 b	12 c	16 c	20 b

Computations:

11 $\$220,000 \div 40,000 = \$5.50$ per hour (c)

12 $\$5.50 \times 44,000 = \$242,000$ (c)

13 $\$242,000 - \$240,000 = \$2,000$ overapplied (a)

14 $\$190,000 - \$10,000 = \$180,000$ (c)

15 $\$790,000 - (\$515,000 - \$10,000) = \$790,000 - \$505,000 = \$285,000$ (a)

II   1 base for applying overhead, 2 (a) direct materials, (b) work in process, (c) finished goods, 3 budgeted factory overhead cost by budgeted direct labor cost or by budgeted machine-hours (or budgeted labor-hours), 4 predetermined overhead rate by the actual amount of the rate base, 5 (a) work in process, (b) finished goods, (c) cost of goods sold.

III   Apogee Products Company

1. (a) $40,000 + 160,000 - 150,000 = \$50,000$
   (b) $32,000 + 150,000 + 190,000 + 148,000 - 498,000 = \$22,000$
   (c) $36,000 + 498,000 - 496,000 = \$38,000$
2. $496,000 + (153,000 - 148,000) = 496,000 + 5,000 = \$501,000$
3. $750,000 - 501,000 = \$249,000$

IV   Ceiling Fans, Inc.

1. (a) Divide budgeted factory overhead cost by budgeted machine-hours: $\$80,000 \div 50,000$ hrs $= \$1.60$ per hour.
   (b) Multiply the actual machine-hours used by the predetermined overhead rate: 55,000 hrs $\times$ $\$1.60 = \$88,000$.
   (c) Subtract the applied factory-overhead cost incurred from the actual factory-overhead cost: $\$88,000 - \$85,000 = \$3,000$ overapplied overhead.
2. Factory department overhead   3,000
      Cost of goods sold   3,000

V   Special Appurtenances Company

Sales	$800,000
Cost of goods sold at normal cost	$530,000
Less overapplied overhead	12,000
Cost of goods sold at actual cost	$518,000
Gross profit	$282,000
Less selling and administrative expenses	210,000
Net income	$ 72,000

PROCESS-COSTING SYSTEMS

MAIN FOCUS AND OBJECTIVES

The preceding chapter described manufacturing costs in general and the *job-cost system* in particular. This chapter deals with the other basic system for costing products—*process costing.* The key concept is *equivalent units produced,* the measure of the amount of work done in a process.

Your learning objectives are to be able to use this concept in computing the *cost of work completed in a process* and the *cost of ending work in process* by each of two process costing methods:

- *weighted-average method*
- *first-in, first-out method (FIFO)*

The only sure path to the attainment of these objectives is conscientious pencil pushing in solving practice problems.

REVIEW OF KEY IDEAS

A. See the textbook diagram in **Exhibit 14-1** for a graphic comparison of the two basic systems of product costing:
   1. **Job-order costing** is appropriate when different products are manufactured in identifiable batches called **jobs.**
   2. **Process costing** is appropriate when uniform product units are manufactured in a continuous flow through a series of standard operations called **processes.**
   3. Be sure to note the flow of costs through the T-accounts shown in this exhibit.

B. Meaning and purpose of **equivalent units produced:**
   1. This key figure measures the amount of work done in a process in terms of **units fully processed** during a given period.
   2. This measurement is made for the primary purpose of computing **costs per product unit,** for example:

a. Material cost per unit in Process 1:

$$\frac{\text{Cost of material used}}{\text{Equivalent units produced}}$$

b. Conversion cost per unit in Process 1:

$$\frac{\text{Conversion costs incurred}}{\text{Equivalent units produced}}$$

C. Computing equivalent units produced:
  1. Let WIP = work in process inventory.
  2. Let PC = percentage of cost completion of WIP at the date of the inventory.
  3. Then, for each factor of production within each process:

Units completed and transferred out	**XXX**
Add: ending WIP units × PC	**XXX**
(a) Equivalent units, weighted-average method	**XXX**
Deduct: beginning WIP units × PC	**XXX**
(b) Equivalent units, FIFO method	**XXX**

  4. Try to understand the logic of these computations and be sure you can relate lines (a) and (b) above to two important textbook exhibits:
    a. **Exhibit 14-4,** "work done to date" (weighted-average method)
    b. **Exhibit 14-6,** "work done in current period only" (FIFO method)

D. A systematic approach that is helpful in making process-cost calculations involves five easy steps:
  1. Summarize in terms of units the physical quantities of production inflows and outflows.
  2. Compute equivalent units of production.
  3. Summarize the total costs to be accounted for.
  4. Compute the appropriate unit costs.
  5. Use these unit costs to allocate and reconcile the total costs of goods completed and ending work in process.

E. Two alternative **cost-flow assumptions** are available for computing unit costs: weighted average and first-in, first-out (FIFO).
  1. The **weighted-average method** treats the beginning inventory of work in process as though it were begun and finished during the current period.

> **See textbook Exhibits 14-5 and 14-9**

    a. Beginning-inventory costs for each type of cost are mingled with the respective current costs.
    b. These costs include **transferred-in costs** (or **previous-department costs**), as well as the present department's costs of material, labor, and overhead.
    c. Therefore the **divisor** for computing unit costs is the **total work done;** that is, the equivalent units that include the previous work on the beginning inventory as well as the current work.
    d. Thus, monthly unit costs actually represent **weighted averages** of beginning-inventory costs and current costs.
  2. The **first-in, first-out method (FIFO)** treats the beginning inventory of work in pro-

cess as though it were a batch of goods separate and distinct from goods started and finished by a process within the same period.

> **See textbook Exhibits 14-7 and 14-11**

    a. Thus, beginning-inventory costs are **not** mingled with current costs.
    b. Therefore the **divisor** for computing unit costs includes **only the equivalent units for the current period** and **not** the equivalent units of work done on the beginning inventory in previous periods.
    c. As a result, monthly unit costs represent only the work that was actually done during the **current period.**
    d. However, when costs are transferred out of one process to the next process or to finished-goods inventory, a **single unit cost** is used that is a weighted average of beginning-inventory costs and currently incurred costs.
  3. Generally, the weighted-average and FIFO methods arrive at about the same product costs.
    a. However, if material prices are volatile, there may be significant differences in results between these two methods.

PRACTICE TEST QUESTIONS AND PROBLEMS WITH SOLUTIONS

I For each of the following multiple-choice and true-false statements, select the most appropriate answer and enter its identification letter in the space provided:

_____ 1. The primary purpose for computing equivalent units produced is to compare the volume of production for individual manufacturing processes: (a) true, (b) false.

_____ 2. When new materials are added to the second process in a series of three manufacturing processes, the journal entry would include: (a) a credit to the second process, (b) a credit to the first process, (c) a debit to the first process, (d) a debit to material inventory, (e) none of these.

_____ 3. When costs for the month are transferred from Process C to Process D, a debit should be made to work in process for Process D: (a) true, (b) false.

_____ 4. In process cost calculations, the completion percentages or fractions for inventories typically pertain to the conversion costs of: (a) the present department, (b) the preceding departments, (c) the present department and all preceding departments, (d) none of these.

_____ 5. Conceptually, the weighted-average method of process costing is closer to job-costing than the FIFO method: (a) true, (b) false.

_____ 6. The costs of the beginning inventory of work in process are mingled with current costs in making unit-cost calculations by: (a) the first-in, first-out method, (b) the weighted-average method, (c) both of these, (d) neither of these.

_____ 7. The unit costs developed by the FIFO process costing method would be more sensitive to current operating influences than the unit costs developed by the weighted-average method: (a) true, (b) false.

_____ 8. When work is transferred from one process to the next process, the cumulative manufacturing costs to that point would be used to obtain an average cost per unit, whether the FIFO or weighted-average method is used: (a) true, (b) false.

_____ 9. When the FIFO process costing method

is used on a monthly basis, the Finished Goods account should be charged at a different unit cost for each batch of product completed within each month: (a) true, (b) false.

___ 10. In comparison with the FIFO method of computing equivalent units produced, the weighted-average method would never result in a lower quantity: (a) true, (b) false.

___ 11. The calculation of equivalent units for conversion costs would always be the same by the FIFO and weighted-average methods if there is no beginning inventory of work in process: (a) true, (b) false.

___ 12. Assume that at the beginning of the second manufacturing process some new raw materials are added. The equivalent units produced for this cost element would always be the same by the FIFO method as the equivalent units for transferred-in costs: (a) true, (b) false.

___ 13. New materials for 700 product units were introduced at the beginning of Process B during a certain month. One thousand product units were completed and transferred out. If the inventory in process consisted of 500 units at the beginning of the month and 200 at the end, compute the equivalent units produced for materials by the weighted-average method: (a) 1,200, (b) 500, (c) 700, (d) some other amount.

___ 14. New materials for 1,050 product units were introduced at the beginning of Process B during a certain month. One thousand product units were completed and transferred out. If the inventory in process consisted of 460 units at the beginning of the month and 510 at the end, compute the equivalent units produced for materials by the FIFO method: (a) 1,510, (b) 460, (c) 1,050, (d) some other amount.

___ 15. A certain process had a beginning inventory of 500 units that were 60 percent completed as to conversion costs and an ending inventory of 200 units that were 30 percent completed. Units started were 2,200, and units completed were 2,500. Compute the equivalent units produced by the weighted-average method: (a) 2,260, (b) 2,560, (c) 2,400, (d) some other amount.

___ 16. A certain process had a beginning inventory of 400 units that were 30 percent completed as to conversion costs and an ending inventory of 600 units that were 40 percent completed. Units started were 2,000 and units completed were 1,800. Compute the equivalent units produced by the FIFO method: (a) 1,920, (b) 1,760, (c) 2,040, (d) some other amount.

___ 17. No new materials are entered in Process Two. The ending inventory of work in process consists of 50 units that are 60 percent completed in Process Two. Compute the total cost of this inventory if unit costs for the month are $8.00 for conversion costs and $10.00 for transferred-in costs: (a) $900, (b) $540, (c) $700, (d) some other amount.

II Given for the B-4 manufacturing process for March:

Inventory in process, January 1, 40% completed	300 units
Transferred into process in January	600 units
Completed and transferred out of process in January	700 units
Inventory in process, January 31, 50% completed	200 units
January 1 inventory costs:	
Transferred-in costs	$3,900
Conversion costs	$2,800
Current costs charged in January:	
Transferred-in costs:	$5,100
Conversion costs	$3,600

No materials are added in this process.

Using the **weighted-average** unit-cost method, calculate the cost of work transferred out in March and the cost of the March 31 inventory of work in process:

Step 1—Summarize physical units

_____
_____
_____
_____
_____
_____

Step 2—Compute output in equivalent units	Transferred-in Costs	Conversion Costs

Step 3—Summarize total costs to account for	Transferred-in Costs	Conversion Costs	Total Costs

Step 4—Compute unit costs	Transferred-in Costs	Conversion Costs	Total Unit Cost

Step 5—Compute total costs of work completed and in process

_____
_____
_____
_____
_____

III Given for the FI manufacturing process for February:

Inventory in process, February 1, 75% completed	200 units
Transferred into process in February	600 units
Completed and transferred out of process in February	500 units
Inventory in process, February 28, 50% completed	300 units

February 1 inventory costs:
Transferred-in costs	$2,200
Conversion costs	$1,300

Current costs charged in February:
Transferred-in costs:	$6,000
Conversion costs	$4,000

No materials are added in this process.

Using the **first-in, first-out** unit-cost method, calculate the cost of work transferred out in February and the cost of the February 28 inventory of work in process:

Step 1—Summarize physical units

_____

_____

_____

_____

_____

_____

Step 2—Compute output in equivalent units	Transferred-in Costs	Conversion Costs

Step 3—Summarize total costs to account for	Transferred-in Costs	Conversion Costs	Total Costs

Step 4—Compute unit costs

	Transferred-in Costs	Conversion Costs	Total Unit Cost

Step 5—Compute total costs of work completed and in process

CHAPTER 14 SOLUTIONS TO PRACTICE TEST QUESTIONS AND PROBLEMS

I

1 b	4 a	7 a	10 a	13 a	16 a
2 e	5 b	8 a	11 a	14 c	17 d
3 a	6 b	9 b	12 a	15 b	

Computations:

13 $(1,000 - 500) + 200 + 500 = 1,200$; or $1,000 + 200 = 1,200$ (a)

14 $(1,000 - 460) + 510 = 1,050$ (c)

15 $(2,500 - 500) + (500)(40\%) + (200)(30\%) + (500)(60\%) = 2,560$; or $2,500 + (200)(30\%)$
    $= 2,560$ (b)

16 $(1,800 - 400) + (400)(70\%) + (600)(40\%) = 1,400 + 280 + 240 = 1,920$ (a)

17 $(60\%)(50)(\$8) + (50)(\$10) = \$240 + \$500 = \$740$ (d)

II   B-4 manufacturing process:

Step 1—Units of physical flow

Work in process, beginning	300 (40%)	Units completed	700
Units transferred in	600	Work in process, end	200 (50%)
Units to account for	900	Units accounted for	900

Step 2—Equivalent units

	Transferred-in Costs	Conversion Costs
Completed and transferred out	700	700
Ending work in process: 200 × 100%	200	
200 × 50%		100
Equivalent units produced	900	800

Step 3—Summary of total costs to account for

	Transferred-in Costs	Conversion Costs	Total Costs
Work-in-process, beginning	$ 3,900	$ 2,800	$ 6,700
Current costs	5,100	3,600	8,700
Total costs to account for	$ 9,000	$ 6,400	$15,400

Step 4—Unit costs

	Transferred-in Costs	Conversion Costs	Total Unit Cost
Total costs to account for (Step 3)	$ 9,000	$ 6,400	
Divide by equivalent units (Step 2)	900	800	
Unit costs	$ 10.00	$ 8.00	$ 18.00

Step 5—Total costs of work completed and in process

Units completed: (700)($18)		$12,600
Work-in-process, end:		
Transferred-in costs: (200)($10)	$2,000	
Conversion costs: (200)(50%)($8)	800	2,800
Total costs accounted for		$15,400

III FI manufacturing process:

Step 1—Units of physical flow

Work-in-process, beginning	200 (75%)
Units transferred in	600
Units to account for	800
Units completed and transferred out during February	500,
Work in process, end	300 (50%)
Units accounted for	800

Step 2—Equivalent units

	Transferred-in Costs	Conversion Costs
Completed and transferred out	500	500
Ending inventory in process: 100% × 300	300	
50% × 300		150
Total work done to date	800	650
Less beginning inventory in process: 100% × 200	200	
75% × 200		150
Equivalent units produced	600	500

Step 3—Summary of total costs to account for

	Transferred-in Costs	Conversion Costs	Total Costs
Work in process, beginning	$ 2,200	$ 1,300	$ 3,500
Current costs	6,000	4,000	10,000
Total costs to account for	$ 8,200	$ 5,300	$13,500

Step 4—Unit costs

	Transferred-in Costs	Conversion Costs	Total Unit Cost
Current costs only	$ 6,000	$ 4,000	
Divide by equivalent units (Step 2)	600	500	
Unit costs	$ 10.00	$ 8.00	$ 18.00

Step 5—Total costs of work completed and in process

Units completed:		
From beginning inventory (Step 3)		$ 3,500
Current costs added:		
Conversion costs: (200)($8)(100% − 75%)		400
Total from beginning inventory		$ 3,900
Started and completed: (500 − 200)($18)		5,400
Total costs transferred out (Average unit cost: $9,300 ÷ 500 = $18.60)		$ 9,300
Work-in-process, end:		
Transferred-in costs: (300)($10)	$3,000	
Conversion costs: (300)(50%)($8)	1,200	4,200
Total costs accounted for		$13,500

OVERHEAD APPLICATION: DIRECT AND ABSORPTION COSTING

MAIN FOCUS AND OBJECTIVES

Much of this chapter relates to the difference between two approaches to income measurement: *direct costing* and *absorption costing*. The essence of this difference is the treatment of *fixed factory-overhead* costs as either:

- *noninventoriable (period) costs by direct costing* or
- *inventoriable (product) costs by absorption costing*

In addition, the chapter gives particular emphasis to the nature and effects of the *production-volume variance* for fixed overhead costs. Learn the meaning of this variance and how to compute it.

REVIEW OF KEY IDEAS

A. There are two major approaches in the application of costs to products for measuring net income:

1. The full-costing, functional, or traditional approach uses **absorption costing.**

   a. **Fixed manufacturing overhead costs** are treated initially as **product costs** and therefore are **included in product inventories** and cost of goods manufactured and sold, along with direct material, direct labor, and **variable** manufacturing overhead costs.

   b. Absorption costing must be used for income tax purposes and is generally accepted for making financial reports to external parties.

2. The contribution approach to income measurement uses **direct costing,** more accurately called **variable costing** or **marginal costing.**

   a. **Fixed manufacturing overhead costs** are treated immediately as **expense** and therefore are **excluded from product inventories,** which include only direct material, direct labor, and **variable** factory-overhead costs.

   b. Direct costing is growing in use for internal performance reports to management, but it is not acceptable for income tax purposes or external reporting.

3.
> **Question: What is the essential difference between these two costing methods?**
>
> **Answer: Timing of the inclusion in expense of fixed manufacturing overhead costs.**

4. This answer is clarified by **textbook Exhibit 15-1.** Note carefully these two main ideas:

   a. In absorption costing, fixed manufacturing overhead is **first included in inventory** and therefore is treated as an **unexpired cost** (an **asset**) until the period in which the inventory is sold and included in cost of goods sold (an **expense**).

   b. However, in direct costing, fixed manufacturing overhead is regarded as an **expired cost** and is **charged against sales immediately,** only **variable** manufacturing costs being included in product inventories.

4. These two approaches produce different reported figures for net income.

> **See textbook Exhibits 15-2 and 15-3**

   a. Notice that when the **quantity of inventory increases** during a period (19X7), direct costing will generally report **less net income** than absorption costing.

   b. However, when the **quantity of inventory decreases** during a period (19X8), direct costing will generally report **more net income** than absorption costing.

   c. You should also note that the absorption-costing approach treats as **expenses** the **production-volume variances** in fixed factory overhead.

B. Two principal purposes of an accounting system are the **control-budgeting** purpose and the **product-costing** purpose.

   1. Accomplishing these two purposes for **variable** costs is less difficult than for **fixed** costs.

      a. This is because, as the volume of production increases, the total **variable** costs rise proportionately.

      b. Therefore graphs for each of these purposes would show the same slope for the total variable costs, as illustrated by the **first pair of textbook graphs.**

   2. On the other hand, to accomplish the control-budgeting purpose and the product-costing purpose for **fixed** costs, one must make separate analyses:

      a. For control-budgeting purposes, total fixed costs may be plotted on a graph as a straight horizontal line.

      b. However, for absorption-product-costing purposes, because fixed costs are applied on a **unit** basis, they would be plotted with a slope to show increases in proportion to volume increases (as though they had a **variable** cost behavior pattern).

      c. These different purposes are reflected by the **second pair of textbook graphs.**

C. To obtain a single standard product cost for pricing and inventory uses, one must select an appropriate activity or volume level, which in our book we call the **denominator volume.**

   1. A predetermined rate for applying fixed factory overhead is then computed for a given year:

$$\text{Budgeted rate} = \frac{\textbf{Budgeted fixed overhead}}{\textbf{Denominator volume}}$$

2. The denominator volume selected can have a significant effect on fixed overhead rates and standard unit costs.
3. However, such rates and unit costs **have limited significance for control purposes.**
4. A **production-volume variance** arises whenever the actual activity deviates from the denominator level.
   a. When actual activity is **less** than the denominator volume, the fixed overhead production-volume variance is **unfavorable.**
   b. The reverse relationship is **favorable** because this would indicate better-than-expected use of facilities.
   c. However, most companies consider such variances to be beyond immediate management control.
   d. Moreover, the production-volume variance depends on the amount of applied fixed overhead, but this is **artificial** for product-costing purposes because it treats a fixed cost as though it were a variable cost.

D.

> **Question: What are the three basic ways for applying costs to products by the absorption-costing approach?**
> **Answer: Actual costing, normal costing, and standard costing. See the short, but helpful comparison table in the textbook.**

E. In addition to the production-volume variance, there can be other variances of actual costs from standard costs.
1. These typically include variances for direct material, direct labor, and variable manufacturing overhead.
2. When the standards are viewed as being **currently attainable,** such variances are often **unfavorable.**
   a. In some cases, these variances would be prorated over inventories and costs of goods sold, thus resulting in inventory valuations that are more representative of the ''actual'' costs of obtaining the products.
   b. However, in practice, these variances are usually treated as **expired costs** and used to adjust current income, as shown in Exhibit 15-7.
   c. Ordinarily, they are **not prorated to unexpired costs** and treated as adjustments to the inventory asset appearing in the balance sheet, because inventory valuations should represent only the **desirable and attainable costs,** not actual costs that may include inefficiencies.

PRACTICE TEST QUESTIONS AND PROBLEMS WITH SOLUTIONS

I For each of the following multiple-choice and true-false statements, select the most appropriate answer and enter its identification letter in the space provided:

_____ 1. More useful for managerial control and decision making is: (a) the absorption-costing approach, (b) the direct-costing approach.

_____ 2. The direct-costing method is not generally acceptable for external financial reporting purposes: (a) true, (b) false.

_____ 3. The absorption-costing method is not acceptable for income tax purposes: (a) true, (b) false.

_____ 4. Both the absorption-costing and direct-costing methods are generally acceptable for internal reporting purposes: (a) true, (b) false.

_____ 5. Fixed factory overhead costs are properly included in product inventories by: (a) the absorption-costing method, (b) the direct-costing method, (c) both of these, (d) neither of these.

_____ 6. Variable factory-overhead costs and variable selling expenses are properly included in product inventories under: (a) the direct-costing method, (b) the absorption-costing method, (c) both of these, (d) neither of these.

_____ 7. Treated immediately as expenses by the direct-costing method are: (a) variable factory-overhead costs, (b) fixed factory-overhead costs, (c) both of these, (d) neither of these.

_____ 8. In its first year of operations, a company produced 20,000 units of a uniform product and sold 18,000 units. Selected data include: direct materials used $80,000, direct labor $150,000, and manufacturing overhead $100,000 (half fixed, half variable). There is no ending inventory of work in process. Compute the ending inventory of finished goods if the absorption-costing method is used: (a) $33,000, (b) $66,000, (c) $23,000, (d) $28,000, (e) some other amount.

_____ 9. See the preceding test item. Compute the ending inventory of finished goods if the direct-costing method is used: (a), (b), (c), (d), (e).

_____ 10. See item 8 above. Compared with the absorption-costing method, the direct-costing method would measure an operating income that is: (a) $10,000 higher, (b) $5,000 lower, (c) $5,000 higher, (d) $10,000 lower, (e) the same amount.

_____ 11. The direct-costing and absorption-costing approaches usually produce the same periodic measurements of net income: (a) true, (b) false.

_____ 12. Amerada Co. manufactured 6,000 units of a uniform product in its first year of operations and sold 5,000 of these units for $500,000. Variable manufacturing costs were $240,000 and fixed factory overhead was $120,000. Selling and administrative expenses were $100,000 fixed and $60,000 variable. Ignore ending inventory of work in process and compute gross profit: (a) $40,000, (b) $140,000, (c) $200,000, (d) none of these.

_____ 13. See the preceding test item and compute the contribution margin: (a) $200,000, (b) $250,000, (c) $240,000, (d) none of these.

_____ 14. Predetermined rates for fixed factory overhead are quite useful for management control purposes: (a) true, (b) false.

_____ 15. The production-volume variances in fixed factory-overhead costs that occur in the absorption-costing approach should be reported as: (a) assets, (b) liabilities, (c) expenses, (d) none of these.

_____ 16. Most companies consider production-volume variances to be within immediate management control: (a) true, (b) false.

_____ 17. When standards are viewed as being currently attainable, variances for direct material, direct labor, and variable factory overhead are often favorable: (a) true, (b) false.

II Complete each of the following statements:

1. The absorption-costing method would tend to report higher profits than would the direct-costing method when the quantity of inventory _____

_____

during a period.

2. If fixed costs are applied on a unit basis, the total amount applied would _____

in proportion to _____ .

3. The predicted activity or volume level for the year may be called _____ .

4. In practice, unfavorable variances for direct material, direct labor, and variable factory overhead are treated as _____ .

III Given for the first year of operations of Mariposa Products, a manufacturer of a uniform product:

	Fixed	Variable
Direct labor cost	$ —	$140,000
Selling and administrative expenses	20,000	50,000
Direct materials used	—	100,000
Factory overhead	72,000	36,000

The company manufactured 12,000 units and sold 9,000 of these units for $360,000. There was no ending inventory of work in process. Compute these amounts:

1. Ending inventory of finished goods:
   (a) Absorption-costing method .... $ _____

   (b) Direct-costing method .... $ _____

2. Gross profit on sales .... $ _____

3. Contribution margin .... $ _____

4. Operating income:
   (a) Absorption-costing method .... $ _____

   (b) Direct-costing method .... $ _____

IV The following information pertains to the operations of Papillon Corporation:

Budgeted fixed overhead cost	$180,000
Denominator level of activity	300,000 hrs.

1. Compute the standard rate for applying fixed overhead:

2. Compute the fixed-overhead production-volume variance if the actual activity level is 280,000 hours:

3. State how this production-volume variance would be shown in an absorption-costing income statement:

4. Compute the fixed-overhead production-volume variance if the actual activity level is 306,000 hours:

5. State how this production-volume variance would be shown in an absorption-costing income statement:

V Given for Farfala Corporation for 19X7:

Beginning inventory	none
Production	10,000 units
Sales at $25 each	8,000 units
Ending inventory	2,000 units
Standard manufacturing costs per unit:	
Variable manufacturing costs	$12
Fixed factory overhead	4
Total	$16
Selling and administrative expenses:	
Variable	$25,000
Fixed	15,000
Total	$40,000

1. Prepare an income statement, using absorption costing, ignoring income taxes, and assuming no production-volume variance:

Sales _____ $ _____

_____ _____

_____ _____

_____ _____

_____ _____

_____ _____

_____ _____

_____ _____

_____ _____

_____ _____

_____ _____

_____ _____

_____ _____

_____ _____

_____ _____

Net income _____ $ _____

2. Prepare an income statement, using direct costing and ignoring income taxes:

Sales _____ $ _____

_____   _____

_____   _____

_____   _____

_____   _____

_____   _____

_____   _____

_____   _____

_____   _____

_____   _____

Net income _____ $ _____

3. Reconcile the difference in net income shown by these two methods:

_____ $ _____

_____   _____

CHAPTER 15 SOLUTIONS TO PRACTICE TEST QUESTIONS AND PROBLEMS

I
1 b	3 b	5 a	7 b	9 d	11 b	13 c	15 c	17 b
2 a	4 a	6 d	8 a	10 b	12 c	14 b	16 b	

Computations:

8 $20,000 - 18,000 = 2,000$ units of ending inventory, which is 10% of production; 10% (80,000 + 150,000 + 100,000) = 10% × 330,000 = $33,000 (a)

9 10% (80,000 + 150,000 + 1/2 × 100,000) = 10% × 280,000 = $28,000 (d)

10 33,000 − 28,000 = $5,000 lower (b); or 10% × 1/2 × 100,000 = 10% × 50,000 = $5,000 (b)

12 Ending inventory is (1,000 ÷ 6,000) = 1/6 of production; ($240,000 + $120,000) = $360,000; $360,000 − 1/6($360,000) = $300,000 cost of goods sold; $500,000 − $300,000 = $200,000 gross profit (c)

13 $240,000 − 1/6($240,000) = $200,000; $500,000 − $200,000 − $60,000 = $240,000 contribution margin (c)

II 1 increases, 2 increase in proportion to volume increases (or change in proportion to volume changes), 3 the denominator volume, 4 expenses or expired costs.

III Mariposa Products

1. The ending inventory is 12,000 − 9,000 = 3,000 units.
    This is 3,000 ÷ 12,000 = 25% of production.
    (a) 25% (140,000 + 100,000 + 36,000 + 72,000) = 25% (348,000) = $87,000
    (b) 25% (140,000 + 100,000 + 36,000) = 25% (276,000) = $69,000
2. Cost of goods sold is 348,000 − 87,000 = $261,000.
    Gross profit is 360,000 − 261,000 = $99,000.
3. Variable cost of goods sold is 276,000 − 69,000 = $207,000.
    Total variable expenses are 207,000 + 50,000 = $257,000.
    Contribution margin is 360,000 − 257,000 = $103,000.
4. (a) 99,000 − (20,000 + 50,000) = 99,000 − 70,000 = $29,000
    (b) 103,000 − (20,000 + 72,000) = 103,000 − 92,000 = $11,000
Proof: Profit difference 29,000 − 11,000 = $18,000 = 87,000 − 69,000 = 25% (72,000) = $18,000

IV Papillon Corporation

1. The standard rate is $180,000 divided by 300,000 hours = 60¢ per hour.
2. Production-volume variance is: (300,000 − 280,000) × 60¢ = $12,000 U.
3. It would be shown in the income statement as a **deduction** from gross profit at standard.
4. Production-volume variance is (306,000 − 300,000) × 60¢ = $3,600 F.
5. It would be shown in the income statement as an **addition** to gross profit at standard.

V   Farfala Corporation

1. Absorption-costing income statement:

Sales: 8,000 units @ $25		$200,000
Less standard cost of goods sold:		
Cost of goods manufactured at standard: 10,000 units @ $16	$160,000	
Less ending inventory: 2,000 units @ $16	32,000	128,000
Gross profit at standard		$ 72,000
Less selling and administrative expenses:		
Variable expenses	$ 25,000	
Fixed expenses	15,000	40,000
Net income		$ 32,000

2. Direct-costing income statement:

Sales: 8,000 units @ $25		$200,000
Variable manufacturing cost of goods produced:		
10,000 units @ $12	$120,000	
Less ending inventory: 2,000 units @ $12	24,000	
Variable manufacturing cost of goods sold: 8,000 units @ $12	$ 96,000	
Variable selling and administrative expenses	25,000	
Total variable expenses		121,000
Contribution margin		$ 79,000
Less fixed costs:		
Factory overhead: 10,000 units @ $4	$ 40,000	
Selling and administrative expenses	15,000	55,000
Net income		$ 24,000

3. Reconcilation of difference in net income:

Net income difference: $32,000 − $24,000		$ 8,000
Ending inventory difference: 2,000 units × ($16 − $12) = 2,000 × $4 fixed		
overhead cost per unit		$ 8,000

QUANTITATIVE TECHNIQUES USED IN MANAGEMENT ACCOUNTING

MAIN FOCUS AND OBJECTIVES

This chapter introduces some important mathematical approaches for use in management planning and control. At the minimum, managers and accountants must be able to recognize appropriate situations for using these approaches. In particular, managerial accountants should be able to:

- *Construct and use decision tables involving probabilities and expected values*
- *Develop linear-programming models and interpret the optimal solution*
- *Set up and use various models for inventory planning and control*

REVIEW OF KEY IDEAS

A. **Decision theory** refers to a systematic approach to making all kinds of decisions.
  1. Such an approach often involves the fields of statistics, mathematics, economics, and psychology, but **accountants** usually provide much of the quantitative data needed in making decisions within organizations.
  2. The key device used is called a **model,** which pictures the principal relationships among the critical factors in a real situation.
     a. Such decision models are typically expressed in mathematical forms.

> Question: Do mathematical models reflect with absolute precision all of the relevant variables?
>
> Answer: No. Although they may not provide perfect answers, such models nevertheless often help in making better decisions.

3. The basic approach to decision theory has five characteristics:
    a. A **choice criterion,** or **objective function,** which is a maximization (or minimization) of some form of profit (or cost) for the purpose of evaluating courses of action and thus assisting in the selection of the best alternative.
    b. A set of **alternative courses of action** that are collectively exhaustive and mutually exclusive.
    c. A set of all relevant **events,** sometimes called **states,** that are also collectively exhaustive and mutually exclusive.
    d. A set of **probabilities** of occurrence of the various events.
    e. A set of **outcomes,** often called **payoffs,** that measure the consequences of the possible combinations of actions and events.
4. The basic elements of a formal decision model are best understood through an example as summarized in the expanded **decision table** in the textbook.

B. Decisions may be made under certainty or under uncertainty.
    1. When decisions are made **under certainty,** for each action there is only one event and therefore only one outcome for each action.
        a. The decision consists of choosing the action that will produce the best outcome.
        b. However, this could be quite difficult if there are a great number of possible actions to consider.
    2. On the other hand, there are many situations involving **uncertainty** where for each action there are **several events,** each with its probability of occurrence.
        a. Decisions are sometimes said to be made **under risk** when these probabilities can be **determined objectively,** either by mathematical proofs or by actual experience.
        b. Decisions are made **under uncertainty** when such probabilities can be assessed only on a **subjective basis.**
        c. However, we use risk and uncertainty as interchangeable terms.
    3. When decisions are to be made under risk or uncertainty, it is often helpful to make some selected computations for a probability distribution.

See textbook Exhibit 16-1

---

    a. The **expected value** of an action is the total of the outcomes of its events, each weighted by its probability of occurrence (the sum of the products of outcomes and probabilities). Be sure you are able to compute expected value.
    b. The **standard deviation,** which is the common measure of the dispersion of a probability distribution, is the square root of the mean of the squared deviations from the expected value.
    c. The **coefficient of variation,** which is a relative measure of risk or uncertainty, is the standard deviation divided by the expected value.
    4. The textbook example of the pastry retailer shows clearly how expected-value calculations are used to determine the action that promises to **maximize payoff** under conditions of uncertainty.
    5. It is sometimes feasible to compute by a popular technique the **value of additional information** that may be available to the decision maker at some cost, as illustrated for the pastry retailer.

See textbook Exhibit 16-2

---

    a. The first step is to prepare a **decision table** for arriving at the **expected value with perfect information** (the total expected value of actions selected on the assumption of perfect prediction of events).

    b. Second, compute the **expected value with existing information** (the expected value of the action that would **maximize payoff** under conditions of uncertainty).

    c. Third, subtract (b) from (a) to arrive at the **expected value of perfect information** (the maximum amount that should be paid for perfect advance information).

C. **Linear programming** is a mathematical search procedure for finding the optimum solution to certain types of problems.

    1. The objective of linear programming is to determine the combination of scarce resources that maximizes profits or minimizes costs.

    2. Practical applications include blending gasoline, routing production, and making shipping schedules.

    3. Linear programming requires that all relationships be **linear** and is most useful when **many combinations** are possible, but it is a decision model under conditions of **certainty.**

    4. The textbook illustration of product mix shows the three basic steps of the linear-programming approach:

        a. Formulate the model.

> **Make sure that you can construct in mathematical form: (1) the equation for the objective function and (2) the inequalities to reflect the constraints of scarce resources.**

        b. Use a computer to identify feasible alternatives and the optimum solution (textbook Exhibit 16-4).

        c. Analyze the solution, including **shadow prices.**

    5. The textbook example uses a graphic plot in conjunction with manual computations to reach the optimum solution.

> **See textbook Exhibit 16-3**

        a. Although the graphic approach is practicable only in the simplest of situations, it is quite useful in understanding the basic concepts of linear programming. Study it carefully.

        b. Most linear-programming problems require digital computers for performing a step-by-step process called the **simplex method.**

D. **Inventory planning and control systems** have as their main objective the determination and maintenance of the **optimum amount of investment in inventory.**

    1. Too much inventory produces large carrying costs, obsolescence risks, and lower rates of return on investment.

    2. On the other hand, if insufficient inventory is carried, costs could result from lost sales and production interruptions.

    3. The cost of purchasing or manufacturing the inventory is usually **not relevant** to the type of inventory-control decisions we are studying, because the total annual requirements are the **same** for various alternatives.

4. There are two classes of costs that **are relevant,** however:
   a. Costs of **ordering** inventories, for example, purchasing, receiving, transportation.
   b. Costs of **carrying** inventories, for example, storage, taxes, insurance, decline in value of inventory.
   c. Specifically, our objective is to **minimize the total of these costs.**

E. One of the two key factors in applying inventory policy is the determination of the **economic order quantity (EOQ),** the optimum size of a normal purchase order for replenishing materials or a shop order for a production run.

See textbook Exhibit 16-6

1. The economic order quantity may be estimated by computing the annual carrying cost and the annual purchase order cost (or setup cost) for each of several selected order sizes. The order size with the **least total cost** would be the approximate economic order quantity.
2. The economic order quantity may be computed more quickly and more accurately by a formula:

$$E = \sqrt{\frac{2AP}{S}}$$

3. If the relevant costs are plotted on a simple graph, the actual order quantity to be used may be conveniently selected from the optimum range, within which the total cost curve tends to flatten (see Exhibit 16-7).

F. The other key factor in applying inventory policy is the determination of the **reorder point,** the quantity level that automatically triggers a new order.

See textbook Exhibit 16-8

1. The inventory reorder point depends on several factors.
   a. The **economic order quantity** was described above.
   b. The **lead time** is the time interval between placing an order and receiving delivery.
   c. The **demand during lead time** is the expected usage during lead time.
   d. The **safety stock** is the estimated minimum inventory quantity needed as a buffer or cushion against reasonable expected maximum usage.
2. The inventory reorder point is commonly computed as the safety stock plus expected usage during lead time.
3. In addition to the reorder point approach, which features a **constant order quantity at variable dates or intervals,** another widely used model is the **constant order-cycle system:**
   a. The reorder date or interval is **fixed.**
   b. However, the quantity ordered **varies** according to the usage since the previous order and the currently expected demand during the lead time.

PRACTICE TEST QUESTIONS AND PROBLEMS WITH SOLUTIONS

I For each of the following multiple-choice and true-false statements, select the most appropriate answer and enter its identification letter in the space provided:

_____ 1. When decisions are made under certainty, there is: (a) only one event for each action, (b) only one outcome for each action, (c) both of these, (d) neither of these.

_____ 2. When decisions are determined under risk, the relevant probabilities can be determined objectively: (a) by mathematical proofs, (b) by actual experience, (c) either of these, (d) neither of these.

_____ 3. The sets of probabilities in mathematical decision models pertain to the likelihood of occurrence of: (a) courses of action, (b) outcomes, (c) events, (d) the objective function, (e) none of these.

_____ 4. When the relevant probabilities can be determined objectively, decisions are said to be made under: (a) certainty, (b) uncertainty, (c) risk, (d) all of these, (e) none of these.

_____ 5. A company developed three predictions of its sales for the next year: optimistic $700,000 with a probability of .20, most likely $500,000 with a probability of .55, and pessimistic $300,000 with a probability of .25. Predicted sales would be: (a) $1,500,000, (b) $500,000, (c) $700,000, (d) $300,000, (e) some other amount.

_____ 6. See the preceding test item. The $700,000 is an example of: (a) an event, (b) a course of action, (c) a state of nature, (d) an outcome.

_____ 7. See item 5 above. "Pessimistic" is an example of: (a) a payoff, (b) a course of action, (c) an event, (d) an outcome.

_____ 8. The coefficient of variation is a relative measure of: (a) efficiency, (b) profitability, (c) accuracy or reliability, (d) risk or uncertainty.

_____ 9. The expected value of perfect information is the excess of the expected value with existing information over the expected value with perfect information: (a) true, (b) false.

_____ 10. The objective of linear programming is: (a) to measure the quality of production, (b) to control the quality of production, (c) to forecast completion dates for special projects, (d) to determine the best combination of production resources.

_____ 11. The prime objective of inventory control is: (a) to decrease opportunities for improper use of inventory, (b) to maximize clerical accuracy in inventory documents and records, (c) to achieve the optimum level of investment in inventory, (d) none of these.

_____ 12. The optimum size of a material purchase order is the size that would minimize the annual purchase order cost: (a) true, (b) false.

_____ 13. The economic order quantity is the quantity that would minimize the annual inventory carrying cost: (a) true, (b) false.

_____ 14. The inventory reorder point would tend to be increased by: (a) a decrease in the expected usage of material during lead time, (b) an increase in the expected usage of material during lead time, (c) neither of these.

_____ 15. The quantity of the safety stock plus expected usage during lead time is equal to: (a) optimum inventory balance, (b) economic order quantity, (c) inventory reorder point.

_____ 16. The constant order-cycle system uses: (a) a fixed reorder interval and a variable order quantity, (b) a fixed order quantity and a variable reorder interval, (c) a variable reorder interval and a variable order quantity, (d) a fixed reorder interval and a fixed order quantity.

II Complete each of the following statements:

1. Typically, mathematical decision models include sets of alternative courses of action, which are collectively _____ and mutually _____ .

2. The payoffs in a mathematical decision model indicate the possible outcomes of _____ _____ for _____ .

3. Decisions are said to be made under risk or uncertainty when there are several _____ _____ , each with its _____ of occurrence.

4. The common measure of the dispersion of a probability distribution is called _____ _____ .

5. The expected value of a particular event is _____ multiplied by _____ _____ .

6. The coefficient of variation is _____ _____ divided by _____ _____ .

7. The mathematical expressions of inequalities for linear-programming problems represent _____ _____ .

8. The optimum level of inventory would minimize _____ _____ .

9. In general, the inventory reorder point is the sum of _____ _____ and _____ .

III Schmetterling & Bee, Ltd., is an oil exploration company. A well is being drilled in the Texas panhandle with the following range of expectations of production per month:

Light producer	.15	$ 80,000
Medium producer	.20	$160,000
Heavy producer	.10	$400,000
Dry hole	.55	-0-

Compute the expected value of production per month: .... $ _____

IV Given for Uranium Discovery Company:

Event	A	B	C	D
Probability of event	.1	.4	.3	.2
Payoffs for actions: 1	$10	$ 5	-0-	−$10
2	$15	$10	$5	−$ 5
3	$20	$15	-0-	-0-
4	$30	$10	-0-	−$15

1. What is the expected value of action 1? .... $_____

2. What is the expected value of action 2? .... $_____

3. What is the expected value of action 3? .... $_____

4. What is the expected value of action 4? .... $_____

5. What is the total expected value with perfect information? .... $_____

6. What is the total expected value of perfect information? .... $_____

V New Orleans Roasters Co. can produce two blends of coffee called Expresso and Eye-Open. The following data are available:

| | Daily Capacity in Units | | Unit Contribution |
Product	Process A	Process B	Margin
Expresso (X)	200	400	$15
Eye-Open (Y)	500	320	$10

Severe material shortages for Expresso will limit its production to a maximum of 180 units per day. Develop appropriate equations for a linear-programming solution:

1. Maximum total contribution margin = _____

2. Process A constraint: _____

3. Process B constraint: _____

4. Material shortage constraint: _____

5. Negative production constraints: _____

VI Given for Material PDQ of Sanger, Inc.:

Total annual requirements .... 8,000 units
Carrying costs per unit per year .... $ 2
Costs per purchase order $80
Inventory level when each order arrives (no safety stock) .... zero

1. Compute the total relevant costs of ordering one, two, five, ten, and twenty times per year:

Number of orders per year	One	Two	Five	Ten	Twenty
Order size	___	___	___	___	___
Average inventory in units	___	___	___	___	___
Yearly ordering costs	$___	$___	$___	$___	$___
Yearly carrying costs	$___	$___	$___	$___	$___
Total relevant costs	$___	$___	$___	$___	$___

2. Check for least-cost order size ___ ___ ___ ___ ___

3. Use the formula for determining the least-cost order size:

VII Given for Material RD-2 of Onward Corporation:

Maximum daily usage	80 units
Expected daily usage	70 units
Minimum daily usage	60 units
Lead time	22 days

1. Compute the safety stock .... _____ units

2. Determine the reorder point .... _____ units

CHAPTER 16 SOLUTIONS TO PRACTICE TEST QUESTIONS AND PROBLEMS

I

1 c	4 c	7 c	10 d	13 b	16 a
2 c	5 e	8 d	11 c	14 b	
3 c	6 d	9 b	12 b	15 c	

Computations:

5 $(.20 \times 700,000) + (.55 \times 500,000) + (.25 \times 300,000) = 140,000 + 275,000 + 75,000 = \$490,000$ (e)

II   1 exhaustive, exclusive, 2 specific courses of action, specific events, 3 events (or states), probability, 4 the standard deviation, 5 its outcome or payoff, its probability of occurrence, 6 the standard deviation, the expected value, 7 the constraints or limiting factors, 8 the total relevant costs of inventories, 9 the expected usage during lead time and the safety stock.

III   Schmetterling & Bee, Ltd.

$.15 \times \$\ 80,000 = \$12,000$
$.20 \times \$160,000 = \ \ 32,000$
$.10 \times \$400,000 = \ \ 40,000$
$.55 \times \ \ \ \ \ \ \ \ \ 0 = \ \ \ \ \ \ \ \ 0$

Expected value $\$84,000$

IV   Uranium Discovery Company

1. $(.1)(10) + (.4)(5) + (.3)(0) + (.2)(-10) = 1 + 2 + 0 - 2 = \$1.00$
2. $(.1)(15) + (.4)(10) + (.3)(5) + (.2)(-5) = 1.5 + 4 + 1.5 - 1 = \$6.00$
3. $(.1)(20) + (.4)(15) + (.3)(0) + (.2)(0) = 2 + 6 + 0 + 0 = \$8.00$
4. $(.1)(30) + (.4)(10) + (.3)(0) + (.2)(-15) = 3 + 4 + 0 - 3 = \$4.00$
5. $(.1)(30) + (.4)(15) + (.3)(5) + (.2)(0) = 3 + 6 + 1.5 + 0 = \$10.50$
6. Item 5 minus item 3 $= \$10.50 - \$8.00 = \$2.50$

V   New Orleans Roasters Co.

1. Maximum total contribution margin: $15X + 10Y$
2. Process A constraint: $X + .4Y \leqslant 200$; or $2.5X + Y \leqslant 500$
3. Process B constraint: $X + 1.25Y \leqslant 400$; or $.8X + Y \leqslant 320$
4. Material shortage constraint: $X \leqslant 180$
5. Negative production constraints: $X \geqslant 0$ and $Y \geqslant 0$

VI Material PDQ of Sanger, Inc.

	One	Two	Five	Ten	Twenty
1. Number of orders per year	One	Two	Five	Ten	Twenty
Order size (8,000 divided by number of orders per year)	8,000	4,000	1,600	800	400
Average inventory in units (order size divided by 2)	4,000	2,000	800	400	200
Yearly ordering cost (number of orders multiplied by $80)	$ 80	$ 160	$ 400	$ 800	$1,600
Yearly carrying cost (average inventory multiplied by $2)	$8,000	$4,000	$1,600	$ 800	$ 400
Total relevant costs	$8,080	$4,160	$2,000	$1,600	$2,000
2. Least-cost order size				X	

3.

$$E = \text{least-cost order size} = \sqrt{\frac{2AP}{S}}$$

A = annual quantity used in units 8,000
P = cost of placing an order $80
S = annual cost of carrying one unit one year $2
  Substitute in formula:

$$E = \sqrt{\frac{2 \times 8,000 \times 80}{2}} = \sqrt{640,000} = 800 \text{ units per order.}$$

Optimum number of orders per year: 8,000/800 = 10 (as above).

VII Material RD-2 of Onward Corporation

1. Maximum daily usage .... 80 units
   Less expected daily usage .... 70 units
   Excess usage per day .... 10 units
   Multiply by lead time .... 22 days
   Safety stock .... 220 units
2. Safety stock .... 220 units
   Added expected usage during lead time; 70 units for 22 days .... 1,540 units
   Reorder point (inventory level at which additional units should be ordered) .... 1,760 units
   Or, the reorder point may be computed as the maximum usage during lead time: 80 units for 22 days .... 1,760 units

BASIC ACCOUNTING: CONCEPTS, TECHNIQUES, AND CONVENTIONS

MAIN FOCUS AND OBJECTIVES

Your main study targets are the three principal financial statements issued by business corporations for the use of their stockholders, creditors, and other external parties:

- *balance sheet*
- *income statement*
- *statement of retained income*

To understand these formal reports, you must be able to analyze typical business transactions and determine their effects on the net income and financial position of a company.

REVIEW OF KEY IDEAS

A. Through the financial accounting process, the accountant accumulates data on the operations of an organization for use by managers, investors, and other interested groups.
   1. The focus is on the entity and its transactions.
      a. An **entity** is a specific area of accountability. The principal form of business entity is the corporation, which is owned by its stockholders.
      b. **Transactions** are events that affect the financial position of an entity and require recording by the entity.
   2. Accountants summarize transactions in the form of two main financial reports:
      a. The **balance sheet,** also called the **statement of financial position,** summarizes at a given **date** the economic resources owned by a company (**assets**) and the claims against them (**equities**).
      b. The **income statement** summarizes for a given **period** the profit-seeking operations of a company in order to measure **net income:** the excess of sales (**revenues**) over the costs of obtaining them (**expenses**).
      c. These two financial statements have a definite relation to each other, because the

net income reported in the income statement for a given period increases the owners' equity, which is shown in the balance sheet at the end of the period.

B. The accounting process records the transactions and events of the **entity,** which may be a business unit, often referred to as a **firm, company,** or **corporation.**

See textbook Exhibits 17-1 and 17-2

---

1. A useful framework for analyzing the financial effects of transactions is the fundamental **balance sheet equation:**

$$\textbf{Assets} = \textbf{Equities, or}$$

$$\textbf{Assets} = \textbf{Liabilities} + \textbf{Owners' Equity}$$

    a. **Assets** are the economic resources owned by the entity, for example, money, merchandise, and machinery.
    b. **Equities** are the claims against, or interests in, the assets.
    c. **Liabilities** are the debts owed to creditors by the company.
    d. **Owners' equity** measures the investment interest of owners and is the excess of a company's assets over its liabilities. For a corporation, this is called **stockholders' equity.**

2. Conscientiously trace the transactions through the analyses provided by Exhibits 17-1 and 17-2.

C. Net income is generally measured on the **accrual basis of accounting,** that is, by **matching related revenues and expenses by periods.**
    1. Revenues are **realized** (recognized in the accounting records and formal financial statements) provided that:
        a. The goods or services sold are "fully rendered" (delivered to customers).
        b. An actual exchange of resources has occurred (in terms of either cash or credit).
        c. There is a reasonable assurance of the conversion of any related assets into cash (collectibility of receivables).
    2. Expenses are **incurred** (recognized in the accounting records and formal financial statements) as goods or services are used to obtain revenues.
        a. Expenses generally cause decreases in assets.
    3. The accrual basis of accounting should be distinguished from the **cash basis** of accounting.

Question: Does the cash basis match revenues and expenses by periods?
Answer: No. The accounting recognition of revenues and expenses would depend on the timing of the related cash receipts and disbursements, thus ignoring the effects on net income of the related liabilities and noncash assets.

D. It is helpful to view assets as **bundles of economic services** held for future use.
    1. When unexpired or stored costs, such as merchandise inventory and equipment, are used in the production of revenue, the expired cost portions are transferred from assets to expenses, which are summarized in the income statement.
    2. In practice, however, some costs are not charged to assets when they are acquired but

are charged immediately to expenses because they measure services that are consumed in a short period of time, for example, advertising expense and interest expense.

E. At the end of an accounting period, in order to complete the implementation of the accrual method, the accountant must make **adjustments** for some implicit transactions that are mostly the result of the passing of time.

1. Formal entries for these adjustments must be made in the accounting records at the end of an accounting period before the financial statements are constructed.

2. The adjustments form an essential element of the accrual basis because they increase the precision of measurements and help provide more complete and realistic reports of operations and financial position.

3. The principal adjustments are classified into four distinctive types:
    a. Expiration of unexpired costs
    b. Realization (earning) of unearned revenues
    c. Accrual of unrecorded expenses
    d. Accrual of unrecorded revenues

4. Examples of the first type include write-offs to expense of the expiration of such assets as office supplies inventory and prepaid fire insurance.

5. **Realization of unearned revenues** means the earning of revenues previously collected in advance.
    a. When cash collections are made in advance by sellers for certain types of services to be rendered later to their customers, these **explicit transactions** create **liabilities** of the sellers called **unearned revenues,** for example, rent collected in advance and insurance premiums collected in advance (unearned insurance premiums).
    b. As time passes, the services are rendered to customers, and **periodic adjustments** must therefore be made to reflect the **implicit transactions,** the decreases in these liabilities and the increases in such revenues as rent earned and insurance premiums earned.

6. **Accrual of expenses** means incurring expenses and accumulating the related liabilities as time passes or as some services are continuously acquired and used.
    a. Common examples are wages, salaries, commissions, taxes, interest on money borrowed, utilities such as electricity, and other operating expenses that are ordinarily not paid in cash until **shortly after** the consumption of the services.
    b. **Periodic adjustments** are made for the **implicit transactions** to increase expenses and the corresponding liabilities for the amounts accrued and not yet entered in the accounting records.

7. **Accrual of revenues** means earning revenues and accumulating the related assets as time passes or as some services are continuously rendered to customers.
    a. Common examples are interest on money loaned, fees for services rendered, and other revenues that are ordinarily not collected in cash until **shortly after** they have been earned.
    b. **Periodic adjustments** are made for the **implicit transactions** to increase revenues and the corresponding assets for the amounts accrued and not yet earned in the accounting records.

F. The finished products of the accounting process are the formal financial statements.

See textbook Exhibits 17-3, 17-4, 17-5

---

1. The **income statement** may show a single-step deduction of expenses from revenues

in determining net income, or the statement may use a multiple-step approach in arriving at the net income figure:

    a. **Gross profit** (or **gross margin**) is the excess of sales over the cost of goods sold.

    b. **Net income** is the gross profit minus operating expenses.

2. **The balance sheet** summarizes an entity's assets, liabilities, and owners' equity.

    a. For a corporation, the owners' equity is divided into two main elements.

    b. One of these is called **contributed capital** or **paid-in capital.** This includes **capital stock,** which usually measures the investment paid in to the corporation by its shareholders.

    c. The other element is called **retained income, retained earnings,** or **reinvested earnings.** This is the **accumulated increase** in the stockholders' equity caused by the total net income earned since the company was formed less **all dividends** paid to stockholders during that time.

> **Question: Is retained income a cash or a noncash asset?**
>
> **Answer: Neither. Retained income is part of the stockholders' equity and therefore is not cash or any kind of asset. Moreover, retained income is not a measure of cash or any other particular asset.**

3. Generally, **dividends** are distributions of cash to stockholders that decrease the company's retained income.

    a. Don't make the serious mistake of confusing dividends with expenses. Dividends are not the cost of producing revenues.

    b. Expenses are deducted from revenues to arrive at net income, which in turn is added to retained income.

    c. Dividends are deducted **directly** from retained income because they represent asset withdrawals that reduce the ownership claims against the business entity.

> **Question: Do dividends decrease net income or retained income?**
>
> **Answer: No for net income, yes for retained income.**

4. For partnerships and sole proprietorships, the equity of each individual owner is measured, but the distinction between contributed capital and retained income is seldom reported.

G. When independent auditors express their opinion of the fairness of a company's financial statements, they specify whether the statements conform to **generally accepted accounting principles (GAAP).**

    1. GAAP have evolved over many years from widespread usage.

        a. This usage has been significantly influenced by the APB, FASB, and SEC.

        b. In essence, although the rule-making power lies with the federal government through the SEC, most of the current rulings are made by the FASB, an independent nongovernmental entity.

    2. An important accounting principle is **realization,** the accounting recognition of revenues when goods or services are delivered to customers (see C1 of this review outline).

    3. Another important principle is the **periodic matching of revenues and expenses,** as represented by the accrual basis of accounting (see C1, C2, and C3 of this outline).

    4. A third important principle is the assumption that we use the **monetary unit** as a **stable**

measure of the financial or economic effects of transactions. This assumption is, of course, subject to serious challenge today in the face of continued inflation.

5. The **going-concern (continuity) assumption** views the business entity as continuing indefinitely with no intention to sell all of its assets and discontinue operations.

6. The **principle of objectivity** or **verifiability** requires accounting measurements to be unbiased, supported by convincing evidence, subject to independent check, and therefore reliable.

7. The **materiality convention** permits relatively small dollar amounts to be accounted for and reported in an expedient manner (even though some basic accounting theory might be ignored).

8. The **cost-benefit idea** means that the benefits from increased precision in accounting for and reporting business transactions must be weighed against the costs of achieving the benefits.

9. These and other GAAP are important guidelines that still permit the use of **considerable judgment** in measuring financial data.

H. In Appendix 17B we take a more technical look at the accounting process.
   1. **Accounts** are used to accumulate the effects of transactions on the **individual items** that are summarized by the terms in the balance sheet equation.
      a. Increases in **asset** accounts are recorded on the left side, decreases on the right.
      b. Increases in **equity** accounts are recorded on the right side, decreases on the left.
      c. An entry on the **left** side of **any account** is called a **debit** or **charge**.
      d. An entry on the **right** side of **any account** is called a **credit**.
      e. The **balance** of an account is the excess of the sum of the dollar entries on one side of the account over the sum of the dollar entries on the other side.
   2. **To understand the use of the debit-credit rules in analyzing the effects of transactions on the accounts and financial statements, carefully follow through the example in this chapter appendix.**

PRACTICE TEST QUESTIONS AND PROBLEMS WITH SOLUTIONS

I For each of the following multiple-choice and true-false statements, select the most appropriate answer and enter its identification letter in the space provided:

____ 1. The two main parts of the owners' equity section of a corporation's balance sheet are: (a) liabilities and stockholders' equity, (b) paid-in capital and liabilities, (c) retained income and paid-in capital, (d) retained income and stockholders' equity.

____ 2. Corporate financial statements are basically the responsibility of the corporation's: (a) stockholders, (b) top management, (c) independent accountants, (d) private (internal) accountants.

____ 3. The independent auditor's opinion accompanying the financial statements is designed to: (a) improve the financial position of the company, (b) ensure the accuracy of data in the statements, (c) relieve the top corporate management of legal liability for misleading financial statements, (d) aid external readers in assessing the credibility of the statements.

____ 4. Revenues are defined as: (a) all flows of incoming cash (cash receipts), (b) net income or net profit, (c) gross increases in assets from delivering goods or services to customers.

____ 5. Martinez Co. purchased merchandise on account for $75,000. As a result, there was: (a) no change in the total amount of its assets, (b) no change in its total liabilities, (c) an increase in the total amount of its assets, (d) an increase in its stockholders' equity.

6. Sandino Co. purchased merchandise with $48,000 of its cash. As a result, there was: (a) no change in the total amount of its assets, (b) an increase in its stockholders' equity, (c) an increase in the total amount of its assets, (d) a decrease in its stockholders' equity.

7. Kinard Co. has total assets of $210,000 and stockholders' equity of $140,000. It purchased $30,000 of merchandise on account and collected $10,000 on account from its debtors. As a result, the company's total liabilities would be: (a) $100,000, (b) $40,000, (c) $240,000, (d) $230,000.

8. See the preceding test item. The company's total assets would be: (a) $250,000, (b) $230,000, (c) $200,000, (d) none of these.

9. The equities shown in the balance sheet of an entity are: (a) the economic resources of the entity, (b) items of property owned by the entity, (c) both of these, (d) neither of these.

10. Maher Co. has $150,000 of liabilities and $350,000 of stockholders' equity. It issued for cash 10,000 shares of $5 par common stock for $20 per share, and purchased land and buildings for $300,000, paying $30,000 cash and signing a note for the balance. As a result, the company's total assets would now be: (a) $1,000,000, (b) $850,000, (c) $950,000, (d) none of these.

11. See the preceding test item. The company's total equities would now be: (a) $420,000, (b) $770,000, (c) $970,000, (d) none of these.

12. Unexpired costs are called: (a) revenues, (b) expenses, (c) losses, (d) assets.

13. Expired costs are called: (a) negative revenues, (b) expenses, (c) liabilities, (d) net losses.

14. The dividends declared and paid by a corporation to its stockholders affect a corporation's financial position as follows: (a) decrease retained income and increase cash, (b) increase retained income and decrease cash, (c) decrease retained income and decrease cash, (d) increase retained income and increase cash.

15. Retained income is an asset: (a) true, (b) false.

16. Items typically reported in a statement of retained income include: (a) net income, (b) dividends to stockholders, (c) both of these, (d) neither of these.

17. Jablonsky Print Co. purchased a large printing press for $300,000, paying $50,000 cash and signing a four-year note for $250,000. As a result, the total amount of the company's assets was: (a) increased by $300,000, (b) decreased by $50,000, (c) increased by $250,000, (d) none of these.

18. Stein's Delivery Service, Inc. purchased merchandise on account for $20,000. It also sold some of its transportation equipment at cost for $120,000, receiving $20,000 in cash and a note for the remainder. As a result, there would be: (a) no change in the total amount of the company's assets, (b) an increase of $20,000 in its assets, (c) a decrease of $20,000 in its assets, (d) a decrease of $80,000 in its assets.

19. The periodic-matching principle requires the matching of expenses with related revenues during a given period: (a) true, (b) false.

20. A company could operate during a given period, earn a net income, and yet suffer a decrease in its cash balance during that period: (a) true, (b) false.

21. A company could operate at a net loss during a given period and yet increase its cash balance during that period: (a) true, (b) false.

22. A company can increase its total assets without earning a net income: (a) true, (b) false.

Based on Appendix 17B:

23. Credit entries are used to record increases in: (a) asset accounts, (b) ex-

pense accounts, (c) both of these, (d) neither of these.

___ 24. An entry on the left side of any account may be called: (a) a debit, (b) a charge, (c) either of these, (d) neither of these.

___ 25. An entry on the right side of any account may be called: (a) a credit, (b) a charge, (c) both of these, (d) neither of these.

II Complete each of the following statements:

1. If a company purchases merchandise inventory on account (for credit), its total assets would be

_____

_____ , its total liabilities would be _____

_____ ,

and its stockholders' equity would be _____

_____ .

2. When unexpired or stored costs, such as merchandise inventory or equipment, are used in the production of revenue, the expired cost portions are

transferred from _____

_____ accounts to _____

_____ accounts, which are

summarized in _____

_____ .

3. Gross profit is the excess of _____

_____ over _____ .

4. The three tests that must be met before revenues may be recognized in the accounting records are:

(a) _____

_____

(b) _____

_____

(c) _____

_____

5. Synonyms for retained income include:

(a) _____

(b) _____

(c) _____

6. The three main organizations that are directly related to the development and enforcement of GAAP are:

(a) _____

(b) _____

(c) _____

Based on Appendix 17B:

7. Decreases in liability accounts are recorded by

_____ entries.

8. An entry on the _____ side of an account is called a credit.

III Use the following data to prepare an income statement and a balance sheet:

Accounts payable	$ 4,000	Depreciation expense	$ 100
Accounts receivable	7,000	Furniture and fixtures	5,100
Accrued interest payable	20	Inventory	4,800
Accrued salaries payable	300	Notes payable	2,000
Advertising expense	200	Prepaid rent	350
Capital stock	18,000	Rent expense	700
Cash	7,650	Retained income	500
Cost of goods sold	5,000	Salaries expense	2,500
Unearned rent revenue	80	Sales	9,000

INCOME STATEMENT

BALANCE SHEET

Assets			Liabilities & Stockholders' Equity		

IV Given the following selected data for Gondola Corporation, compute: (1) net income for 1980, (2) retained income at December 31, 1984.

Retained income at January 1, 1984	$110,000
Cash dividends declared and paid to stockholders in 1984	20,000
All other cash payments in 1984	280,000
Total cash receipts in 1984	315,000
Depreciation expense in 1984	10,000
All other 1984 expenses	235,000
Total revenues for 1984	260,000

V. 1. Complete this transaction analysis framework:

Transaction	Cash	+	Accounts Receivable	+	Merchandise Inventory	+	Prepaid Rent	+	Store Equipment	=	Accounts Payable	+	Paid-in Capital	+	Retained Income
1. Issued capital stock for cash, $100,000															
2. Issued capital stock for store equipment, $50,000															
3. Purchased store equipment for cash, $10,000															
4. Purchased merchandise on account, $70,000															
5. Sold merchandise on account, $35,000															
6. Recorded cost of merchandise sold, $20,000															
7. Sold part of store equipment at cost on account, $2,000															
8. Collected cash on account for previous credit sales recorded, $13,000															
9. Recorded depreciation of store equipment, $1,000															
10. Paid cash for six months' rent in advance, $9,000															
11. Recorded current month's rent expense, $1,500															
12. Paid cash for current month's salaries, advertising, utilities, and miscellaneous office supplies purchased and used, $8,500															
13. Paid cash on account to suppliers for merchandise purchases previously made and recorded, $40,000															
14. Declared and paid cash dividends to stockholders, $3,000															
Totals															

2. Compute: (a) Total assets .... $ _____   (c) Total stockholders' equity ...... $ _____

(b) Total liabilities .... $ _____   (d) Total equities .... $ _____

VI End-of-Period Adjustments. Use only the words **increase, decrease,** or **no effect** to fill each of the blanks below to indicate the usual effect of these end-of-period adjustments on a company's reported assets, liabilities, revenues, and expenses:

	Assets	Liabilities	Revenues	Expenses
1. Expiration of unexpired costs				
2. Realization (earning) of previously deferred revenues				
3. Accrual of previously unrecorded expenses				
4. Accrual of previously unrecorded revenues				
5. Depreciation				

CHAPTER 17 SOLUTIONS TO PRACTICE TEST QUESTIONS AND PROBLEMS

I

1 c	6 a	11 c	16 c	21 a
2 b	7 a	12 d	17 c	22 a
3 d	8 d	13 b	18 b	23 d
4 c	9 d	14 c	19 a	24 c
5 c	10 d	15 b	20 a	25 a

Computations:

7 $210,000 - 140,000 + 30,000 = \$100,000$ (a)

8 $210,000 + 30,000 + 10,000 - 10,000 = \$240,000$ (d)

10 $150,000 + 350,000 + (10,000 \times 20) + (300,000 - 30,000) = \$970,000$ (d)

11 $150,000 + 350,000 + (10,000 \times 20) + (300,000 - 30,000) = \$970,000$ (c). (Remember that total assets equal total equities.)

17 $300,000 - 50,000 = \$250,000$ (c)

18 $20,000 - 120,000 + 20,000 + 100,000 = \$20,000$ (b)

II 1 increased, increased, unchanged, 2 asset, expense, the income statement, 3 sales, cost of goods sold, 4 (a) goods or services must be fully rendered, (b) an exchange of resources evidenced by a market transaction must occur, (c) the collectibility of any noncash assets must be reasonably assured, 5 retained earnings, undistributed earnings, reinvested earnings, 6 (a) Accounting Principles Board (APB), (b) Financial Accounting Standards Boards (FASB), (c) Securities Exchange Commission (SEC), 7 debit, 8 right.

III   INCOME STATEMENT

Revenue:

Sales		$9,000
Expenses:		
Cost of goods sold	$5,000	
Depreciation expense	100	
Rent expense	700	
Advertising expense	200	
Salaries expense	2,500	8,500
Net income (before income taxes)		$ 500

Alternative form of income statement (multiple-step form):

Sales		$9,000
Cost of goods sold		5,000
Gross profit		$4,000
Operating expenses:		
Depreciation expense	$ 100	
Rent expense	700	
Advertising expense	200	
Salaries expense	2,500	3,500
Net income (before income taxes)		$ 500

BALANCE SHEET

Assets		Liabilities and Stockholders' Equity		
Cash	$ 7,650	**Liabilities:**		
Accounts receivable	7,000	Accounts payable		$ 4,000
Inventory	4,800	Notes payable		2,000
Prepaid rent	350	Accrued interest payable		20
Furniture and fixtures	5,100	Accrued salaries payable		300
		Unearned rent revenue		80
		Total liabilities		$ 6,400
		Stockholders' equity:		
		Capital stock	$18,000	
		Retained income	500	
		Total stockholders' equity		$18,500
Total	$24,900	Total		$24,900

IV   Gondola Corporation

1. Revenues		$260,000
Less expenses:		
Depreciation	$ 10,000	
Other expenses	235,000	245,000
Net income		$ 15,000
2. Retained income, January 1, 1984		$110,000
Net income for 1984		15,000
Total		$125,000
Cash dividends for 1984		20,000
Retained income, December 31, 1984		$105,000

V. 1. Transaction Analysis

Transaction	Assets					=	Liabilities & Stockholders' Equity		
	Cash +	Accounts Receivable +	Merchandise Inventory +	Prepaid Rent +	Store Equipment +	=	Accounts Payable +	Paid-in Capital +	Retained Income
1. Issued capital stock for cash, $100,000	+100,000							+100,000	
2. Issued capital stock for store equipment, $50,000					+50,000			+50,000	
3. Purchased store equipment for cash, $10,000	−10,000				+10,000				
4. Purchased merchandise on account, $70,000			+70,000				+70,000		
5. Sold merchandise on account, $35,000		+35,000							+35,000
6. Recorded cost of merchandise sold, $20,000			−20,000						−20,000
7. Sold part of store equipment at cost on account, $2,000		+2,000			−2,000				
8. Collected cash on account for previous credit sales recorded, $13,000	+13,000	−13,000							
9. Recorded depreciation of store equipment, $1,000					−1,000				−1,000
10. Paid cash for six months' rent in advance, $9,000	−9,000			+9,000					
11. Recorded current month's rent expense, $1,500				−1,500					−1,500
12. Paid cash for current month's salaries, advertising, utilities, and miscellaneous office supplies purchased and used, $8,500	−8,500								−8,500
13. Paid cash on account to suppliers for merchandise purchases previously made and recorded, $40,000	−40,000						−40,000		
14. Declared and paid cash dividends to stockholders, $3,000	−3,000								3,000
Totals	42,500	24,000	50,000	7,500	57,000		30,000	150,000	1,000

2. Compute (a) Total assets .... $181,000   (c) Total owners' equity $151,000
           (b) Total liabilities .... $ 30,000   (d) Total equities $181,000

	Assets	**Liabilities**	**Revenues**	**Expenses**
1.	decrease	no effect	no effect	increase
2.	no effect	decrease	increase	no effect
3.	no effect	increase	no effect	increase
4.	increase	no effect	increase	no effect
5.	decrease	no effect	no effect	increase

Chapter 18

UNDERSTANDING CORPORATE
ANNUAL REPORTS—PART ONE

MAIN FOCUS AND OBJECTIVES

This chapter explains the framework and terminology of corporate annual reports. Your general objective is to expand significantly your working vocabulary in the field of financial reporting.

Specifically, you should be able to construct and interpret a corporation's formal *statement of changes in financial position.*

REVIEW OF KEY IDEAS

A. Corporate balance sheets are usually prepared in **classified form** (see textbook **Exhibit 18-1**). Main elements are:
1. **Assets:** the economic resources owned by the corporation:
   a. **Current assets** are the assets directly involved in the **operating cycle** and usually include: cash, temporary investments in marketable securities, accounts receivable less allowance for doubtful accounts, merchandise inventories, and prepaid expenses.
   b. **Property, plant, and equipment** (sometimes called **fixed assets** or **plant assets**) include the original cost of land and the original cost of other long-term tangible assets less accumulated depreciation (cost allocated to expense since acquisition of the assets). The remainder is called **net book value. Leasehold improvements** and **natural resources** are often reported as plant assets.
   c. **Intangible assets** include goodwill, patents, franchises, trademarks, and copyrights. These are reported at original cost, less accumulated amortization where applicable.
2. **Liabilities:** the monetary obligations of the corporation:
   a. **Current liabilities** are company debts falling due within the coming year or within the normal operating cycle if longer than a year. They include: accounts payable

to suppliers, notes payable to banks and others, accrued expenses payable, and federal income taxes payable.

    b.   **Long-term liabilities** fall due beyond the coming year and include mortgage bonds and debentures.

  3. **Stockholders' equity** (also called **ownership equity, capital,** or **net worth**): the owner's residual interest in the business, that is, the excess of total assets over total liabilities:

    a.   **Preferred stock** is the par or stated value paid in by investors who purchased stock with a priority over common stock for periodic dividends or liquidating distributions. Preferred stock usually has a **predetermined dividend rate** with a **cumulative feature** and **no voting rights** in stockholder's meetings.

    b.   **Common stock** is the par or stated value paid in by investors in common stock. Although this stock has **no predetermined dividend rate,** it typically has **voting rights,** an **unlimited potential participation in earnings,** and a **limited liability** for debts owed by the corporation to its creditors.

    c.   **Paid-in capital in excess of par or stated value** was formerly called **surplus** or **paid-in surplus.** This is the excess received by the corporation over the par or stated or legal value of the shares issued.

    d.   **Retained income** (also called **retained earnings** or **reinvested earnings**).

Question: Is retained income an asset?

Answer: No. It is the part of stockholders' equity measured by the excess of accumulated profits over accumulated dividends distributed to stockholders since the company was formed.

---

    e.   In addition to such **positive** elements as the above four items, the stockholders' equity section may include a **negative** item called **treasury stock,** the company's cost of reacquiring some of its own capital stock that had previously been issued.

B.   In accounting, the term **reserve** never means a **fund** or any other kind of asset. Technically, a reserve can be used to refer to any of three quite different kinds of items often appearing in balance sheets:

  1. An **appropriation or restriction of retained income** to inform the reader of the balance sheet that the intent or authority to declare dividends has been restricted by a certain amount for a specified reason.

    a.   Examples include the contingencies of impending lawsuits or currency devaluations.

Question: Does an appropriation of retained income reduce the total amount of retained income?

Answer: No. It is merely an earmarking or segregating or subdividing of part of retained income.

---

  2. An **asset valuation account** (or **asset offset**), for example, such asset deductions as allowance for uncollectible accounts or accumulated depreciation.

  3. An **estimated liability of indefinite or uncertain amount,** for example, such payables as product guarantees, employee pensions, and income taxes.

C.   The income statement reports a company's revenues (sales) and expenses and the net income or net loss that represents the difference between revenues and expenses.

See textbook Exhibit 18-5

1. Note how this **multiple-step income statement** arrives at a figure called **income from operations.**
   a. Interest expense is deducted from this figure.
   b. In this way, the statement reflects the distinction between **operating management** and **financial management.**
2. The face of the income statement must also show the **earnings per share of common stock.**
   a. In the simplest capital structure, the earnings-per-share figure is net income divided by the number of common shares outstanding.

D. The **statement of retained income** reports the effects of net income and dividends on the balance of retained income.

See textbook Exhibit 18-6

1. Net income increases retained income.
2. Dividends to stockholders decrease retained income but are **not expenses** (not deductions in computing net income).

E. The **statement of changes in financial position** is also called the **statement of sources and applications of funds,** or simply the **funds statement.** It typically summarizes the **causes** of changes in **working capital** during a fiscal period, and it must be presented as a basic financial statement in corporate annual reports.

See textbook Exhibit 18-7

1. The basic approach to the construction of the funds statement is to analyze the differences between the figures reported in the company's balance sheets at the beginning and end of a fiscal period.
2. The principal **sources of working capital** are **causes of increase in working capital,** sometimes called **working capital provided:**
   a. **Operations** (revenues, less charges against revenues requiring working capital)
   b. **Sale of noncurrent assets,** such as plant, equipment, and long-term investments in securities
   c. **Issuance of long-term debt,** for example, bonds payable
   d. **Issuance of capital stock**
3. The principal **uses of working capital** are **causes of decreases in working capital,** sometimes called **working capital applied:**
   a. **Declaration of cash dividends**
   b. **Acquisition of noncurrent assets**
   c. **Retirement of long-term debt**
   d. **Purchase of outstanding capital stock** (acquisition of treasury stock)
4. The changes statement is helpful in understanding the major sources and uses of working capital, the causes of changes in working capital, and the policies of a company's top management regarding dividends, expansion, and financing.

F. In the computation of the amount of working capital provided by operations (revenues and expense transactions), **depreciation is often added to net income,** as shown by the first alternative in Schedule A of the textbook Exhibit 18-7.

1. This is done, **not** because depreciation provides or generates working capital, but because depreciation is a **nonfund** type of charge that had been deducted in arriving at net income.

   a. That is, depreciation is a proper expense, but it does not require a **current outlay** of cash or any other element of working capital.

2. The same result could, of course, be achieved simply by omitting depreciation from the list of expenses deducted from sales in determining the working capital provided by operations.

   a. See the second alternative in Schedule A of the textbook Exhibit 18-7.

   b. However, the shortcut method is usually followed in practice (the first alternative in Schedule A).

3. Although it is certainly true that depreciation reduces income taxes, this is also true, of course, for all other deductible expenses of operating a business.

   a. Income taxes, however, are **outflows** of working capital that are taken into account in computing working capital provided by operations.

   b. If an **accelerated depreciation** method is used (for example, the **Accelerated Cost Recovery System**) instead of the straight-line method, the **current** outflows of working capital for income taxes are reduced. (There is a **postponement** of income taxes, but **total** income taxes are **not necessarily reduced** by the use of accelerated depreciation.)

G. Not all companies follow solely the working-capital concept of funds in their statements of changes in financial position.

   1. All companies are now required to disclose **all** the important aspects of financing and investing activities, whether or not cash or other elements of working capital are directly affected, for example, issuance of stock or bonds for noncurrent assets.

   2. Sometimes a statement of sources and applications of **cash** is also used in an annual statement.

See textbook Exhibit 18-8

   3. Study this important exhibit carefully.

PRACTICE TEST QUESTIONS AND PROBLEMS WITH SOLUTIONS

I For each of the following multiple-choice and true-false statements, select the most appropriate answer and enter its identification letter in the space provided:

_____ 1. Current assets include: (a) cash and land, (b) accounts receivable and payable, (c) trademarks and equipment, (d) merchandise inventories and prepaid expenses.

_____ 2. The financial report of Lee & Perrin, Inc. showed a $50,000 increase in current assets and a $40,000 decrease in current liabilities. Thus there was a working-cap-

ital: (a) increase of $10,000, (b) decrease of $10,000, (c) increase of $90,000, (d) none of these.

_____ 3. Depreciation accounting is: (a) a cost allocation process, (b) a valuation process, (c) both of these, (d) neither of these.

_____ 4. The usual balance sheet presentation of property, plant, and equipment shows their: (a) resale value, (b) replacement cost, (c) both of these, (d) neither of these.

_____ 5. Accumulated depreciation is a cash fund

for replacement or expansion: (a) true, (b) false.

____ 6. The intangible asset classification used in financial statements includes: (a) trademarks, (b) accounts receivable, (c) both of these, (d) neither of these.

____ 7. The goodwill asset should be measured by the excess of the fair value of net identifiable assets of businesses acquired over the total purchase price of the businesses acquired: (a) true, (b) false.

____ 8. When a company develops goodwill through advertising, managerial ability, and maintenance of high-quality products and services, the goodwill should be placed on the books and carried as an asset in the balance sheet: (a) true, (b) false.

____ 9. Current liabilities are company debts falling due within the current year or within the normal operating cycle if longer than a year: (a) true, (b) false.

____ 10. If capital stock is issued by a corporation at a price in excess of par or stated value, the excess is a gain that may be reported as part of retained earnings: (a) true, (b) false.

____ 11. When a corporation declares and distributes periodic cash dividends to its stockholders, the results include decreases in the corporation's (a) retained income, (b) stockholders' equity, (c) both of these, (d) neither of these.

____ 12. The cost of treasury stock held by a corporation is: (a) an asset, (b) a negative element of stockholders' equity.

____ 13. The income statement of Schultz and Madeo, Inc. reported $500,000 of sales and $400,000 of total expenses, including $30,000 of depreciation. During the same period, its accounts payable increased by $20,000 while accounts receivable decreased by $6,000 and merchandise inventory increased by $32,000. Compute the working capital provided by operations: (a) $124,000, (b) $136,000, (c) $70,000, (d) $130,000.

____ 14. See the preceding test item and compute the amount of cash provided by opera-

tions: (a) $124,000, (b) $136,000, (c) $70,000, (d) $130,000.

____ 15. In accounting, a reserve may mean: (a) an asset or an estimated liability, (b) an asset offset or a liability offset, (c) an asset offset or an estimated liability, (d) an asset or a liability offset.

____ 16. When retained income is "appropriated," there is a reduction in total stockholders' equity: (a) true, (b) false.

____ 17. Whether a company buys merchandise for cash or credit, the amount of its working capital is not affected: (a) true, (b) false.

____ 18. Sources of working capital would include: (a) acquisition of treasury stock, (b) issuance of capital stock, (c) both of these, (d) neither of these.

____ 19. Uses of working capital would include: (a) retirement of long-term debt, (b) declaration of dividends, (c) both of these, (d) neither of these.

____ 20. The purchase of noncurrent assets: (a) is a use of working capital, (b) increases working capital, (c) both of these, (d) neither of these.

____ 21. The issuance of long-term debt: (a) decreases working capital, (b) increases stockholders' equity, (c) both of these, (d) neither of these.

____ 22. Depreciation is a proper deduction from revenue in arriving at: (a) net income, (b) working capital provided by operations, (c) both of these, (d) neither of these.

____ 23. In computing the amount of working capital provided by operations, one should add depreciation to net income because depreciation: (a) generates funds, (b) provides cash, (c) is not an expense, (d) does not require a current cash outlay.

____ 24. ACRS ignores the terminal values of assets: (a) true, (b) false.

II Complete each of the following statements:

1. The four principal financial statements that appear in annual reports are:

(a) _____

(b) _____

(c) _____

(d) _____

2. The cost of plant and equipment less accumulated depreciation leaves a cost residue commonly called _____ .

3. Retained income, also called _____ _____ or _____ _____ , is the increase in stockholders' equity from the excess of accumulated _____ _____ over accumulated _____ since the company was formed.

4. A company's own capital stock once issued and later reacquired by the company is called _____ .

5. An earmarking of retained income for financial reporting purposes may be called _____ _____ .

6. The issuance of long-term debt is _____ _____ of working capital; it _____ working capital.

7. If uses of working capital exceed sources of working capital for a given company during a certain period, there will be _____ in _____ .

8. The amount of working capital provided by operations is net _____ plus _____ _____ .

III Given for Vick's Trading Company's operations for 19X8 (in thousands):

Total cash receipts	$700
Total cash disbursements	590
Total revenues earned	516
Total expenses incurred (including cost of goods sold)	455
Total dividends declared and distributed to stockholders	40
Additional capital stock issued at par	50
Treasury capital stock acquired at cost	20

1. Compute the net income for 19X8: .... $ _____

2. Compute the net change in retained income for 19X8: .... $ _____

3. Compute the net change in stockholder's equity for 19X8: .... $ _____

IV For each of the transactions listed below for the Multi-Facts Corporation, use plus, minus, or zero symbols to indicate the effect on net income, total owners' equity, and working capital. The first is given as an example.

	Net Income	Total Owners' Equity	Working Capital
1. Issued capital stock for cash	0	+	+
2. Issued capital stock for plant site (land)			
3. Issued capital stock for merchandise inventory			
4. Paid bonds payable with cash			
5. Declared and distributed cash dividends			
6. Recorded bad debt expense			
7. Collected accounts receivable in cash			
8. Paid accounts payable with cash			
9. Purchased land and buildings with cash			
10. Purchased treasury stock with cash, $900			
11. Sold treasury stock in (10) for $700 cash			
12. Created a reserve for contingencies			
13. Created a reserve for depreciation of machinery			
14. Increased bond sinking fund (a noncurrent asset)			
15. Recorded accrued salaries			
16. Purchased merchandise on account			
17. Collected rents in advance in cash			
18. Sold merchandise on account (for credit) at a profit			

V From the following data, prepare a statement of changes in financial position for Flowing Funds Company, using the form that is provided:

	December 31	
	19X2	**19X1**
Current assets	$840,000	$870,000
Current liabilities	150,000	240,000
Land	115,000	130,000
Buildings and Equipment, net	435,000	440,000
Bonds payable	100,000	300,000
Capital stock	550,000	400,000
Retained income	590,000	500,000

	For 19X2 Year
Net income	$160,000
Depreciation	25,000
Dividends on capital stock	70,000
Gain or loss on sale of land	none

FLOWING FUNDS COMPANY

Statement of Changes in Financial Position
For the Year Ended December 31, 19X2

Sources of working capital:

Total sources		

Uses of working capital:

Total uses		
Increase in working capital (Note A)		

Note A:

Working capital, Dec. 31, 19X2		
Working capital, Dec. 31, 19X1		
Increase explained above		

I							
1 d	4 d	7 b	10 b	13 d	16 b	19 c	22 a
2 c	5 b	8 b	11 c	14 a	17 a	20 a	23 d
3 a	6 a	9 a	12 b	15 c	18 b	21 d	24 a

Computations:

2 $\$50,000 + \$40,000 = \$90,000$ (c)

13 $\$500,000 - \$400,000 + \$30,000 = \$130,000$ (d)

14 $\$130,000 + \$20,000 + \$6,000 - \$32,000 = \$124,000$ (a)

II 1 (a) balance sheet (b) income statement (c) statement of retained income, (d) statement of changes in financial position, 2 net book value, 3 retained earnings, reinvested earnings, profits (or earnings, or net income), dividends distributed, 4 treasury stock, 5 an appropriation of retained income, 6 a source, increases, 7 a decrease in working capital, 8 income, charges not requiring working capital.

III Vick's Trading Company

1. Total revenues earned $516
   Less total expenses incurred 455
   Net income .... $ 61
   (Cash receipts and disbursements are not relevant here.)

2. Net income as above .... $ 61
   Less dividends to stockholders 40
   Increase in retained income .... $ 21

3. Increase in retained income as above .... $ 21
   Additional capital stock issued 50
   Total .... $ 71
   Less treasury stock acquired 20
   Increase in stockholders' equity .... $ 51

IV Multi-Facts Corporation

	Net Income	Total Owners' Equity	Working Capital		Net Income	Total Owners' Equity	Working Capital
1	0	+	+	10	0	−	−
2	0	+	0	11	0	+	+
3	0	+	+	12	0	0	0
4	0	0	−	13	−	−	0
5	0	−	−	14	0	0	−
6	−	−	−	15	−	−	−
7	0	0	0	16	0	0	0
8	0	0	0	17	0	0	0
9	0	0	−	18	+	+	+

FLOWING FUNDS COMPANY

Statement of Changes in Financial Position
For the Year Ended December 31, 19X2

Sources of working capital:

Net income	$160,000	
Add depreciation	25,000	
Working capital provided by operations		$185,000
Sale of land ($130,000 − $115,000)		15,000
Issuance of capital stock ($550,000 − $400,000)		150,000
Total sources		$350,000

Uses of working capital:

Purchase of equipment ($435,000 + $25,000 − $440,000)		$ 20,000
Retirement of bonds payable ($300,000 − $100,000)		200,000
Payment of dividends		70,000
Total uses		290,000
Increase in working capital (Note A)		$ 60,000

Note A:

Working capital, Dec. 31, 19X2, $840,000 − $150,000		$690,000
Working capital, Dec. 31, 19X1, $870,000 − $240,000		$630,000
Increase explained above		$ 60,000

UNDERSTANDING CORPORATE ANNUAL REPORTS—PART TWO

MAIN FOCUS AND OBJECTIVES

In Part One of the chapter, your main learning targets are to be able to explain the relationship between *parent* and *subsidiary* companies and to become familiar with *consolidated corporate financial statements.*

In Part Two, your objective is to be able to compute and use some well-known *financial ratios* for analyzing reported corporate data.

REVIEW OF KEY IDEAS

Part One

A. When one company has a long-term investment in the equity securities (capital stock) of another company, there are two methods of accounting for the investment:

1. If the ownership is less than 20%, the **cost method** may ordinarily be used.

   a. The initial investment is recorded at acquisition cost, and dividends received from the investee are treated as income.

   b. Thus the carrying amount of the investment is **unaffected** by the dividends or profits of the investee.

2. If the ownership is 20% to 50%, the **equity method** must ordinarily be used, because it would usually be assumed that the owner has the ability to influence significantly the operations of the investee.

   a. The initial investment is recorded at acquisition cost, but this basis is adjusted for the investor's share of the earnings and losses of the investee after the investment date.

   b. Dividends received from the investee are treated as reductions of the cost basis of the investment.

   c. Under this method, the net income of the investor **could not be directly affected** by manipulating the dividend policies of the investee, because dividends received by the investor are not treated as income.

B. When a corporation owns more than 50% of the outstanding voting shares of another corporation, there is a **parent-subsidiary relationship** that usually results in the operation of these two separate legal entities in the manner of a **single economic unit.** Therefore the financial data of such companies would be combined into **consolidated statements.**

See textbook Exhibit 19-1

1. This means that the assets and equities in the individual balance sheets of the parent and subsidiary companies are **added together** except for the **eliminations of the intercompany items** to avoid double-counting of duplicate items.

    a. Thus the parent company's asset, investment in subsidiary, is canceled against the subsidiary's stockholders' equity (or the appropriate proportion of it).

    b. If part of the subsidiary's capital stock is **not owned** by the parent company (a **minority interest**), the consolidated balance sheet would ordinarily include this outside interest just above the stockholders' equity section.

> **Question: Does this minority interest represent the ownership interest in the parent company or the consolidated group of companies?**
>
> **Answer: Neither. It represents the ownership interest of the minority stockholders in one or more of the subsidiary companies in which they own stock.**

2. In the consolidated income statement, the expenses and revenues of the two companies are also combined, but there would be a deduction for any minority share of subsidiary net income (textbook Exhibit 19-2).

3. Note two important points concerning consolidated statements:

    a. The separate legal entities continue to operate, each with its own set of accounts.

    b. For periodic reporting purposes, the accounts of parent and subsidiary are merely added together, after eliminating double-counting.

4. In some cases, parent and subsidiary companies have markedly different types of businesses (for example, banking and transportation).

    a. In such cases, their financial statements should **not** be consolidated.

    b. The parent company should carry its investment in subsidiary by the **equity method** (as explained above in A2).

C. When one company purchases another, often called a **merger,** the purchasing company should record the assets obtained at **acquisition cost** (the agreed amount of money to be paid, or the fair value of other assets exchanged).

1. If the total purchase price exceeds the sum of the fair value of the identifiable individual assets acquired less the liabilities, the excess, often called **purchased goodwill,** is an asset that should be reported on the consolidated balance sheet as "excess of cost over fair value of net identifiable assets of businesses acquired."

2. Such a goodwill should be carried as a separate intangible asset on the consolidated balance sheet but should be **amortized** (systematically charged to expense) over a period not greater than forty years, because the income-producing ability of goodwill is not likely to last forever.

D. **Financial statement analysis**
1. Purposes:
    a. Evaluating past performance
    b. Predicting future performance
2. Techniques:
    a. Comparing data: with data of similar companies, against industry averages, and through time
    b. Measuring differences from budgets and cash-flow projections
    c. Computing ratios and component percentages to aid in **profit evaluation** and **solvency determination**
3. **Component percentages** are really ratios.

See textbook Exhibit 19-7

---

a. Note how the elements in IBM Corporation's income statement are related to the dollar amount of **sales,** which is used as the **base figure** for the component percentages, for example, net income: $6,700 ÷ $45,800 = 15%.
b. In the balance sheet, the **total asset** dollar amount is used as the **base** for determining the component percentages of the major balance sheet items, for example, stockholders' equity: $26,500 ÷ $42,800 = 62%.

E. The IBM Corporation data are used to illustrate some typical ratios.

See textbook Exhibit 19-8

---

1. **Short-term ratios** help in assessing a company's ability to pay its current debts on time:
    a. **Current ratio:**

$$\frac{\text{Current assets}}{\text{Current liabilities}}$$

    b. **Inventory turnover:**

$$\frac{\text{Cost of goods sold}}{\text{Average inventory at cost}}$$

    c. **Average collection period in days:**

$$\frac{\text{Average accounts receivable} \times 365}{\text{Sales on account}}$$

2. **Debt-to-equity ratios** help in judging the risks of insolvency and disappearance of profits:
    a. **Current debt to equity:**

$$\frac{\text{Current liabilities}}{\text{Stockholders' equity}}$$

b. Total debt to equity:

$$\frac{\text{Total liabilities}}{\text{Stockholders' equity}}$$

3. **Profitability ratios** aid in measuring operating success and overall accomplishment:
   a. **Gross profit rate or percentage:**

$$\frac{\text{Gross profit}}{\text{Sales}}$$

   b. **Return on sales:**

$$\frac{\text{Net income}}{\text{Sales}}$$

   c. **Return on stockholders' equity:**

$$\frac{\text{Net income}}{\text{Average stockholders' equity}}$$

   d. **Earnings per share:**

$$\frac{\text{Net income less preferred dividends}}{\text{Average common shares outstanding}}$$

   c. **Price-earnings ratio:**

$$\frac{\text{Common market price per share}}{\text{Earnings per share}}$$

4. **Dividend ratios** relate profit distributions to common stock prices and earnings:
   a. **Dividend yield:**

$$\frac{\text{Dividends per common share}}{\text{Market price per common share}}$$

   b. **Dividend-payout ratio:**

$$\frac{\text{Dividends per common share}}{\text{Earnings per common share}}$$

5. The analytical value of all these ratios depends heavily on comparisons with data of the same company for other periods and with industry standards.
   a. Study the textbook section **"Discussion of Individual Ratios."**
   b. Note especially the comparison of the IBM Corporation ratios with the Dun and Bradstreet industry statistics.

F. **The pretax operating rate of return on total assets** helps measure operating performance:

$$\frac{\text{Operating income}}{\text{Average total assets available}}$$

1. This ratio can also be computed by multiplying the two following ratios:
   a. **Operating margin percentage on sales:**

$$\frac{\text{Operating income}}{\text{Sales}}$$

b. **Total asset turnover:**

$$\frac{\text{Sales}}{\text{Average total assets available}}$$

2. The understanding and use of this ratio are aided by thus separating it into its basic components.

G. Recent research has indicated that capital markets are **efficient.**
   1. This means that stock market prices "fully reflect" relevant data currently available.
   2. Thus financial ratios and other reported data are, in effect, "translated" by informed readers and analysts so that they have the **same kind of informational impact** on investors, regardless of the different accounting and reporting methods that may be used, assuming, of course:
      a. That there are **adequate disclosures** of such methods, either in the body of the financial statements or in the accompanying footnotes (as required by the SEC and FASB)
      b. That the alternative accounting methods have no underlying effect on the **amounts or timing of cash flows**

PRACTICE TEST QUESTIONS AND PROBLEMS WITH SOLUTIONS

I For each of the following multiple-choice and true-false statements, select the most appropriate answer and enter its identification letter in the space provided:

Part One

____ 1. The carrying amount of one company's long-term investment in the equity securities of another company would be unaffected by the dividends or profits of the investee if: (a) the cost method of accounting were used, (b) the equity method of accounting were used, (c) neither of these.

____ 2. The equity method must generally be used when the equity ownership by one company of another company is less than 20%: (a) true, (b) false.

____ 3. When two companies have a parent-subsidiary relationship: (a) they are separate legal entities, (b) they are a single economic entity, (c) both of these, (d) neither of these.

____ 4. The minority interest measures the interest of: (a) parent company stockholders in the subsidiary company, (b) subsidiary company stockholders in the parent company, (c) neither of these.

____ 5. When parent and subsidiary companies have totally different types of business: (a) their financial statements should not be consolidated, (b) the parent company should carry its investment in the subsidiary by the equity method, (c) both of these, (d) neither of these.

____ 6. When a company develops "goodwill" internally, it should be placed on the books and reported as an asset in the balance sheet: (a) true, (b) false.

____ 7. Purchased goodwill should be: (a) amortized, (b) carried indefinitely without amortization.

____ 8. First Company owns 30% of the voting stock of Second Company, which reported a net income in Year One of $10 million and paid $4 million of cash dividends. Compute the increase in the retained income of First Company in Year One from Second Company's operations, using the **cost** method: (a) $3.0 million, (b) $1.8 million, (c) $1.2 million, (d) some other amount.

_____ 9. See the preceding test item. Compute the increase in the retained income of First Company in Year One from Second Company's operations, using the **equity** method: (a), (b), (c), (d).

_____ 10. See item 8 above. Assume that the acquisition cost of First Company's investment was $100 million. Compute the year-end balance of First Company's investment account, using the equity method: (a) $103.0 million, (b) $101.8 million, (c) $101.2 million, (d) some other amount.

_____ 11. Bigg Company acquired a 90% voting interest in Smal Company for $150 million. The stockholders'equity of Smal Company was $160 million at acquisition, and the book values of its individual assets were equal to their fair market values. Compute the consolidated goodwill: (a) $16 million, (b) $10 million, (c) $6 million, (d) negative $10 million.

_____ 12. See the preceding test item. The minority interest is: (a) $16 million, (b) $15 million, (c) $1 million, (d) negative $15 million.

_____ 13. The individual net incomes of a company and its 75% owned subsidiary were each $16 million. Compute the consolidated net income: (a) $32 million, (b) $20 million, (c) $24 million, (d) $28 million.

Part Two

_____ 14. Nix Co. has a working-capital ratio of two to one. It paid part of its accounts payable. As a result, the working-capital ratio: (a) decreased, (b) increased, (c) was not affected.

_____ 15. The dividend yield multiplied by the price-earnings ratio would be equal to the dividend-payout ratio: (a) true, (b) false.

_____ 16. Normad Co. has $12,000 current assets, $150,000 sales, $75,000 total assets, and $24,000 net income. What is the component percentage for $3,000 accounts payable? (a) 12.5%, (b) 2%, (c) 25%, (d) 4%.

_____ 17. The efficient capital market idea means, for example, that if a company changes from accelerated depreciation to straight-line depreciation for its reports to stockholders, the market price of its stock will tend to: (a) rise, (b) fall, (c) stay the same.

_____ 18. When component-percentage income statements are constructed, the base figure is usually (a) net income, (b) gross profit, (c) total expenses, (d) sales.

_____ 19. Your company's inventory turnover increased. This suggests (a) decreased profitability, (b) better management, (c) greater risk of decline in value of inventory.

_____ 20. The average collection period of accounts receivable decreased. This suggests (a) closer screening of credit applications from customers, (b) increased cash sales, (c) greater risk of uncollectibility of accounts receivable.

II Complete each of the following statements:

Part One

1. Under the equity method of accounting for a parent company's interest in subsidiary, the investment in the subsidiary should be carried as

_____

in the parent company's balance sheet at _____

_____ plus the consolidated group's

share of accumulated _____

_____ since acquisition.

2. When one company buys another, the excess of the total purchase price over the fair values of the identifiable individual assets acquired less the liabilities is often called _____ .
This is an asset that should be reported in the acquiring company's balance sheet as "_____

_____

_____
_____.''

Part Two

3. The pretax operating rate of return on total assets can be computed by multiplying the _____ _____ by the _____.

4. The total asset turnover is _____ divided by average total assets available.

5. The dividend-payout ratio for common stock is _____ divided into _____.

6. The inventory turnover is _____ divided into _____.

7. The average collection period for accounts receivable is 365 days multiplied by (_____ _____ divided by _____).

Part One

III Company P owns 40% of the voting stock of Company S. Given in millions of dollars:

Cost of P's 40% ownership	$180
Net income of S in year one	20
Cash dividends of S in year one	10

Compute:
1. Year-end balance of P's investment account:
   (a) Using the equity method .... $ _____

   (b) Using the cost method .... $ _____

2. Increase in retained income of P in year one from S operations:
   (a) Using the equity method .... $ _____

   (b) Using the cost method .... $ _____

IV Absorption Company acquired 20% of the voting stock of Going Company for $60 million. During the following year, Going reported a net income of $25 million and distributed total cash dividends of $15 million.

1. Assume that the **cost method** is used by Absorption Company. Compute:
   (a) The carrying amount of the investment at the end of the year .... $ _____

   (b) The increase in Absorption's reported stockholders' equity because of subsidiary operations during the year .... $ _____

2. Assume that the **equity method** is used by Absorption Company. Compute:
   (a) The carrying amount of the investment at the end of the year .... $ _____

   (b) The increase in Absorption's reported stockholders' equity because of subsidiary operations during the year .... $ _____

V Lift Company acquired Bootstrap Company. Before the acquisition the companies had neither debt nor preferred stock outstanding. Their annual reports before the acquisition revealed the following data:

	Lift	Bootstrap
Net assets	$80,000	$20,000
Stockholders' equity	80,000	20,000
Net income	8,000	7,000

Lift Company issued capital stock with a market value of $50,000 in exchange for all the stock of Bootstrap Company. Assume that the book value and the current value of the individual assets of Bootstrap were equal before the acquisition.

1. Compute the following for the consolidated company immediately after acquisition:
   (a) Purchased goodwill .... $ _____

   (b) Net assets (including goodwill) .... $ _____

   (c) Stockholders' equity .... $ _____

2. Compute the prospective annual net income of the consolidated company, assuming that purchased goodwill is not to be amortized .... $ _____

3. Compute the prospective annual net income of the consolidated company, assuming that purchased goodwill is to be amortized to expense on a straight-line basis over a five-year period .... $ _____

VI Company P has just acquired a 90% voting interest in Company S for the amount shown below in the investment account (all amounts in millions of dollars):

P Co.:	Investment in S	$180
	Cash and other assets	440
	Liabilities	200
	Stockholders' equity	420
S Co.:	Cash and other assets	500
	Liabilities	300
	Stockholders' equity	200

1. Prepare a consolidated balance sheet. (No work sheet is required, but show support for all figures.) Assume that the book values of S individual assets are equal to their fair market values.

2. Compute the consolidated goodwill, assuming that a 75% voting interest had been acquired, but use all the **same dollar numbers** shown above. Also assume that the book values of the S individual assets are equal to their fair market values. Prepare the consolidated balance sheet (work sheet not required).

Part Two

VII Selected data for Universal Sizing Corporation (in millions):

Sales	$800	Cost of goods sold	$500
Current assets	240	Current liabilities	120
Stockholders' equity	200	Merchandise inventory	125
Accounts receivable	80	Accounts payable	60
Retained income	150	Net income	36

Assume that all sales were on account. Compute each of the ratios indicated below. It is not necessary to compute any average amounts for balance sheet figures.

Current ratio:	_____	to 1
Inventory turnover:	_____	times
Collection period for accounts receivable:	_____	days
Gross profit rate:	_____	%
Return on sales:	_____	%
Return on stockholders' equity:	_____	%

VIII Given for Carousel Corporation (in millions):

Operating income	$ 54
Sales	900
Average total assets available	500

Find:

1. Operating margin percentage on sales .... _____ %

2. Total asset turnover .... _____ times

3. Pretax operating rate of return on total assets .... _____ %

CHAPTER 19 SOLUTIONS TO PRACTICE TEST QUESTIONS AND PROBLEMS

I										
	1 a	3 c	5 c	7 a	9 a	11 c	13 d	15 a	17 c	19 b
	2 b	4 c	6 b	8 c	10 b	12 a	14 b	16 d	18 d	20 a

Computations:

8 $30\% \times 4 = 1.2$ million (c)
9 $30\% \times 10 = 3.0$ million (a)
10 $100 + 30\%(10 - 4) = 100 + 30\% \times 6 = 100 + 1.8 = \$101.8$ million (b)
11 $150 - 90\%(160) = 150 - 144 = \$6$ million (c)
12 $10\% \times 160 = \$16$ million (a)
13 $16 + 75\%(16) = 16 + 12 = \$28$ million (d)
16 $3,000 \div 75,000 = 4\%$ (d)

II   1 an asset, original cost, retained income, 2 purchased goodwill, excess of cost over fair value of net identifiable assets of businesses acquired, 3 multiplying the operating margin percentage on sales by the total asset turnover, 4 sales, 5 common earnings per share divided into common dividends per share, 6 average inventory divided into cost of goods sold, 7 average accounts receivable divided by sales on account.

III   Company P and Company S (in millions of dollars)

1. (a) $180 + 40\%(20 - 10) = 180 + 4 = \$184$
   (b) $180
2. (a) $40\%(20) = \$8$
   (b) $40\%(10) = \$4$

IV   Absorption Company

1. (a) $60 million
   (b) $20\% \times \$15$ million of dividends $= \$3$ million
2. (a) $60 million $+ (20\% \times \$25$ million$) - (20\% \times \$15$ million$) =$
       $60 million $+ \$5$ million $- \$3$ million $= \$62$ million
   (b) $20\% \times \$25$ million $= \$5$ million

V   Lift Company and Bootstrap Company

1.	(a) Market value of capital stock exchanged	$ 50,000
	Less current value of individual assets of Bootstrap	20,000
	Goodwill	$ 30,000
	(b) Net assets of Lift before acquisition	$ 80,000
	Individual assets of Bootstrap before acquisition	20,000
	Goodwill, as above	30,000
	Net assets after acquisition (including goodwill)	$130,000
	(c) Stockholders' equity of Lift before acquisition	$ 80,000
	Market value of additional Lift capital stock issued	50,000
	Stockholders' equity after acquisition	$130,000
2.	Net income of Lift before acquisition	$ 8,000
	Net income of Bootstrap before acquisition	7,000
	Prospective annual net income after acquisition	$ 15,000

3. Prospective annual net income before goodwill amortization, as above .... $ 15,000
   Less goodwill amortization: $30,000/5 yrs. 6,000
   Prospective annual net income after goodwill amortization .... $ 9,000

VI   Company P and Company S

1.

Assets		Liabilities and Stockholders' Equity	
Cash and other assets (440 + 500)	$940	Liabilities (200 + 300)	$500
		Minority interest (10%)(200)	20
		Stockholders' equity	420
Total assets	$940	Total equities	$940

Assets		Liabilities and Stockholders' Equity	
2. Consolidated goodwill: $180 - 75\%(200) = 180 - 150 = \$30$			
Cash and other assets (400 + 500)	$940	Liabilities (200 + 300)	$500
Consolidated goodwill	30	Minority interest (25%)(200)	50
		Stockholders' equity	420
Total assets	$970	Total equities	$970

VII   Universal Sizing Corporation

Current ratio: $240 \div 120 = 2$ to 1 or 200%

Inventory turnover: $500 \div 125 = 4$ times

Collection period: $(80 \times 365) \div 800 = 36.5$ days

Gross profit rate: $(800 - 500) \div 800 = 37.5\%$

Return on sales: $36 \div 800 = 4.5\%$

Return on stockholders' equity: $36 \div 200 = 18\%$

VIII   Carousel Corporation

1. $54 \div 900 = 6\%$ 2. $900 \div 500 = 1.8$ times   3. $54 \div 500 = 10.8\%$
3. alternative calculation: $6\% \times 1.8 = 10.8\%$

Chapter 20

DIFFICULTIES IN MEASURING
NET INCOME

MAIN FOCUS AND OBJECTIVES

Part One of the chapter explains four different ways of measuring the *flow of costs* from inventories to cost of goods sold. Your prime learning target is to gain a working knowledge of the *FIFO* and *LIFO* methods and their effects on the reporting of assets and net income.

In the second part of the chapter, you should acquire some understanding of various ways for coping with *changing price levels* in balance sheets and income statements.

REVIEW OF KEY IDEAS

Part One

A. When identical or similar goods are purchased at different times and prices, four alternative methods are acceptable for measuring the **cost** of inventory: **specific identification, weighted average, FIFO,** and **LIFO.**

> See textbook Exhibits 20-1 and 20-2

1. Essentially, these methods rest upon assumptions concerning the **sequence of cost flows;** that is, the method chosen directly affects the **timing** of the transfer of costs from **assets** (inventories) to **expenses** (costs of goods used or sold).
2. Such assumptions can result in strikingly different amounts reported in financial statements:
    a. Inventory asset in the balance sheet
    b. Net income in the income statement

3. In general, however, the chosen inventory method must be used **consistently** from year to year.
4. **Specific identification** requires a tracing of the actual inventory items through the inventory and into cost of goods sold.
    a. This is usually not feasible except for high-unit-value types of goods, for example, automobiles and expensive jewelry.
    b. Thus the **flow of costs** coincides with the **physical flows** of inventory items.
5. However, the other three methods do **not** require that the flow of costs coincide with the actual sequence of the physical flow of inventory.
6. The **weighted-average** method requires a computation of the **weighted-average unit cost** of goods available for sale.
    a. Such an average is **not a simple average;** it is the total cost of beginning inventory and purchases divided by the total number of units of the beginning inventory and purchases.
    b. This average unit cost is then multiplied by units to arrive at the cost of goods sold, and the cost of the ending inventory.
7. The **first-in, first-out method** (FIFO) assumes that the cost of the earliest-acquired stock is used first, whereas the **last-in, first-out method** (LIFO) makes the opposite assumption.

8. | **Question: Compared with the LIFO method, does the FIFO method leave the ending inventory valuation nearer to current replacement costs?**
    Answer: Yes, but the FIFO method tends to mismatch old costs with current revenues (sales).

9. In contrast, LIFO values the inventory on an old cost basis but tends to match current costs more closely with current revenues, and therefore LIFO measures a net income **that correlates more closely with the increase in assets available for the distribution of dividends to stockholders.**
10. Compared with FIFO, the use of LIFO tends to show lower inventory measurements during periods of rising prices (and higher inventory figures when prices are falling).
    a. If prices are rising, LIFO therefore tends to show less income than FIFO, and thus it often **minimizes current income taxes.** This is the main reason many companies have adopted LIFO.
    b. The use of LIFO also permits management to influence the measurement of net income by deciding on the **timing** of purchases.

Part Two

B. The measurement of net income depends first on the distinction between **capital maintenance** and the **return on capital.**
    1. In turn, this distinction depends on the meaning of capital maintenance; two different meanings exist.
    2. The first is **financial capital maintenance,** the idea that capital is measured in terms of the **money invested** in resources.
        a. This meaning reflects the traditional **historical-cost** view, that is, ignoring the effects of general price inflation.
    3. The second meaning is **physical capital maintenance,** that is, the maintenance of **physical operating capability** in terms of inventory, plant assets, and so forth.

a. This meaning allows for the inclusion of the additional measures of money required for keeping physical facilities intact during general price inflation.

C. Although net income is a widely accepted indicator of the performance of a company for a given period of time, there is considerable disagreement as to how net income should be measured in an inflationary environment. There are four major ways to report income and capital in financial reports.

See textbook Exhibit 20-3

---

1. The conventional **accrual method** of measuring net income matches realized revenues with the expired costs of assets (Method 1 of Exhibit 20-3). This is the generally accepted **historical-cost approach using nominal dollars.** However, it has two serious weaknesses:
   a. The reported data for income and capital **do not reflect changes in current replacement costs** of goods sold and goods in the ending inventory.
   b. The reported data **ignore general price inflation:** the increase in the general price level (decrease in the purchasing power of money).
2. The **current-cost approach using nominal dollars** focuses on **income from continuing operations** (Method 2 of Exhibit 20-3).
   a. Excluded from this income are **holding gains** from goods sold and unsold, these being reported as part of **revaluation equity** (excess of current replacement costs over historical costs).
   b. Holding gains cannot be distributed as dividends without impairing the invested capital needed to maintain **physical capacity.**
3. A less radical way to coping with the measurement distortions of the conventional accrual method is to use general price indexes to adjust the nominal dollars of **historical costs to constant dollars** (Method 3 of Exhibit 20-3).
   a. These adjusted amounts measure **current purchasing power.**
   b. Be sure to note that these are merely **restated costs** and that they are not intended to reflect specific current values.
4. A fourth approach to measuring income and capital is to use general price indexes to convert **current costs to constant dollars** (Method 4 of Exhibit 20-3).
   a. Advocates of this method claim that it is the best way to measure income and capital.
   b. They reason that the financial statements should reflect the **total change in wealth measured in constant dollars, including both realized and unrealized elements.**
5. Although the use of price indexes and current costs can help accountants measure income more realistically and determine whether invested capital has been maintained, it is not yet a common practice to prepare and issue financial statements on these bases.

D. The chapter appendix considers **inflation accounting** in greater depth.
   1. This is a relatively dynamic area of accounting thought having a tremendous potential for influencing basic changes in financial reporting, perhaps in the near future.
   2. Additional terminology, concepts, procedures, and problems are explained and illustrated.
   3. For example, when the term **current cost** is used, this can mean:
      a. Usually: **today's cost** of acquiring a similar asset that would produce the same expected cash flows as the existing asset, often called **replacement cost.**
      b. Sometimes: **net realizable value,** which is the estimated selling price less related costs.

4. When constant dollars are used to measure income (textbook Methods 1 and 3, Exhibit 20-3), a distinction must be made between two types of balance sheet items:
   a. **Monetary items** are fixed claims receivable or payable in a specified number of dollars (or other monetary units). Examples: cash, accounts receivable, bonds payable.
   b. **Nonmonetary items** have variable prices or values in terms of dollars. Examples: inventory, equipment, land, natural resources.
5. During inflationary times, there is a **purchasing-power loss** that must be recognized for monetary items when the constant-dollar methods are used to measure income, but no such loss would be recognized for nonmonetary items.

PRACTICE TEST QUESTIONS AND PROBLEMS WITH SOLUTIONS

I For each of the following multiple-choice and true-false statements, select the most appropriate answer and enter its identification letter in the space provided.

Part One

____ 1. The specific-identification inventory method would probably be most appropriate for (a) a grocery store, (b) a yacht dealer, (c) a cafeteria, (d) a passenger airline.

____ 2. The FIFO inventory method assumes that the cost of the most recently acquired inventory items is represented by the unsold items: (a) true, (b) false.

____ 3. Compared with the FIFO method, LIFO tends to (a) leave the inventory valuation closer to current replacement costs, (b) match current costs more closely with current sales.

____ 4. During a period of rising prices, the use of the LIFO method, in comparison with FIFO, will tend to produce lower reported net income and higher reported cost of goods sold: (a) true, (b) false.

____ 5. The main reason many companies have adopted LIFO is its appeal (a) in matching current costs with current revenues, (b) in measuring net income more conservatively, (c) in minimizing current income taxes.

Part Two

____ 6. The traditional historical-cost view is consistent with: (a) physical capital maintenance but not financial capital maintenance, (b) financial capital maintenance but not physical capital maintenance, (c) both physical and financial capital maintenance, (d) neither physical nor financial capital maintenance.

____ 7. When the historical costs of assets are adjusted by the use of general price indexes, the resultant figures are current costs: (a) true, (b) false.

____ 8. The current-cost approaches exclude accumulated holding gains from: (a) retained income but not stockholders' equity, (b) retained income and stockholders' equity, (c) neither retained income nor stockholders' equity.

____ 9. Accumulated holding gains are not available for dividends without impairing invested capital: (a) true, (b) false.

____ 10. Holding gains are identified in financial data based on: (a) historical costs adjusted by general price indexes, (b) current costs using nominal dollars, (c) neither of these.

____ 11. The current-cost concept of income is based on the physical concept of maintenance of invested capital, not the financial concept of maintenance of invested capital: (a) true, (b) false.

___ 12. During inflationary times, purchasing-power gains and losses could be recognized for: (a) monetary items but not nonmonetary items, (b) nonmonetary items but not monetary items, (c) both monetary nor nonmonetary items, (d) neither monetary nor nonmonetary items.

II Complete each of the following statements:

Part One

1. The three inventory methods that do **not** require that cost flows coincide with the actual sequence of physical flows are

(a) _____

(b) _____

(c) _____

2. The inventory method that assumes that the cost of the oldest inventory items acquired is represented by the current inventory is _____

_____ .

3. During a period of rising prices, the inventory asset will tend to be reported at the highest cost by the _____ method.

Part Two

4. The conventional accrual method for measuring net income values assets on the _____ basis.

5. General price indexes are used to restate _____ _____ costs in terms of _____ purchasing power.

6. Business managers would naturally tend to favor the treatment of holding gains as _____ _____ .

Part One

III Compute for Providence Co. the total cost of the ending inventory by each method indicated.

Given:

Beginning inventory:	30 units at $ 8 each
Purchases: May	40 units at $ 9 each
August	20 units at $10 each
September	50 units at $12 each
Ending inventory:	60 units

(a) FIFO $ _____   (b) LIFO $ _____   (c) Weighted average $ _____

IV Given for Real Profit Company:

	Units	Price	Total
Inventory, January 1, 19X1	100	$200	$20,000
Purchases in 19X1	200	300	60,000
Sales in 19X1	180	500	90,000
Inventory, December 31, 19X1	120		*
Operating expenses in 19X1	—	—	16,000

*To be computed.

1. Complete the following income statements and cash summaries, assuming that all transactions are for cash:

INCOME STATEMENTS

	FIFO Method	LIFO Method
Sales	$ _____	$ _____
Less cost of goods sold:		
Beginning inventory	_____	_____
Purchases	_____	_____
Cost of goods available for sale	_____	_____
Less ending inventory:		
	_____	
	_____	
	_____	
	_____	_____
Cost of goods sold	_____	_____
Gross profit on sales	_____	_____
Less operating expenses	_____	_____
Income before income tax	_____	_____
Less income tax at 60%	_____	_____
Net income for 19X1	$ _____	$ _____

CASH SUMMARIES

	FIFO Method	LIFO Method
Cash payments:		
Purchases	$ _____	$ _____
Operating expenses	_____	_____
Income tax	_____	_____
Total cash payments	_____	_____
Cash receipts	_____	_____
Cash increase (decrease) for 19X1	$ _____	$ _____

2. Which method would tend to induce the greater expectation by stockholders for cash dividends in 19X1? _____ Why? _____

_____

3. Which method would tend to provide the greater ability of the company to pay cash dividends in 19X1? _____ Why? _____

Part Two

V The Moving Horizon Corporation has just been formed, having issued $10,000 of capital stock for cash. It immediately purchased 1,000 units of inventory for cash at $10 per unit. During the first year of operations, it sold 700 units for $20 cash each. At the end of the year, the replacement cost of the inventory was $15 per unit, and the general-price-level index had increased 20% from the beginning of the year. Compute the following amounts for each of the four methods of reporting income and capital. Assume no other transactions, and ignore income taxes.

	Nominal Dollars		Constant Dollars	
	Method 1 **Historical** **Cost**	**Method 2** **Current** **Cost**	**Method 3** **Historical** **Cost**	**Method 4** **Current** **Cost**
1. Income from continuing operations	$ _____	$ _____	$ _____	$ _____
2. Ending inventory	$ _____	$ _____	$ _____	$ _____
3. Retained income	$ _____	$ _____	$ _____	$ _____
4. Original paid-in capital	$ _____	$ _____	$ _____	$ _____
5. Holding gains on units sold .	$ _____	$ _____	$ _____	$ _____
6. Holding gains on units unsold	$ _____	$ _____	$ _____	$ _____
7. Total assets (cash and inventory)	$ _____	$ _____	$ _____	$ _____
8. Total equities (items 3, 4, 5, 6)	$ _____	$ _____	$ _____	$ _____

CHAPTER 20 SOLUTIONS TO PRACTICE TEST QUESTIONS AND PROBLEMS

I
1 b	3 b	5 c	7 b	9 a	11 a
2 a	4 a	6 b	8 a	10 b	12 a

II   1 average, FIFO, and LIFO, 2 LIFO, 3 FIFO, 4 historical cost, 5 historical costs in terms of current purchasing power, 6 revaluation of capital.

III   Providence Co.

(a) $(50 \times 12) + (10 \times 10) = 700$
(b) $(30 \times 8) + (30 \times 9) = 510$
(c) $(30 \times 8) + (40 \times 9) + (20 \times 10) + (50 \times 12) = 1400$; $1400 \div (30 + 40 + 20 + 50) = 1400 \div 140 = 10$; $10 \times 60 = 600$

IV   Real Profit Company

1.
                                    INCOME STATEMENTS

	FIFO	LIFO
Sales	$ 90,000	$ 90,000
Less cost of goods sold:		
Beginning inventory	$ 20,000	$ 20,000
Purchases	60,000	60,000
Cost of goods available for sale	$ 80,000	$ 80,000
Less ending inventory:		
120 units at $300 =	36,000	
100 units at $200 = $ 20,000		
20 units at $300 = 6,000		
Total		26,000
Cost of goods sold	$ 44,000	$ 54,000
Gross profit on sales	$ 46,000	$ 36,000
Less operating expenses	16,000	16,000
Income before income tax	$ 30,000	$ 20,000
Less income tax at 60%	18,000	12,000
Net income for 19X1	$ 12,000	8,000

                                    CASH SUMMARIES

	FIFO	LIFO
Cash payments:		
Purchases	$ 60,000	$ 60,000
Operating expenses	16,000	16,000
Income tax	18,000	12,000
Total cash payments	$ 94,000	$ 88,000
Cash receipts	90,000	90,000
Cash increase (decrease) for 19X1	$ (4,000)	$ 2,000

2. FIFO, because a larger net income would be reported.
3. LIFO, because more cash would be available.

MOVING HORIZON CORPORATION

	Nominal Dollars		Constant Dollars	
	Method 1 Historical Cost	Method 2 Current Cost	Method 3 Historical Cost	Method 4 Current Cost
1. Income from continuing operations:				
Sales: 700 × $20 = $14,000;				
Deduct 700 × $10 = 7,000	$ 7,000			
Deduct 700 × $15 = 10,500		$ 3,500		$ 3,500
Deduct 120% × $7,000 = $8,400			$ 5,600	
2. Ending Inventory:				
300 × $10	3,000			
300 × $15		4,500		4,500
300 × $10 × 120%			3,600	
3. Retained income (same as 1)	7,000	3,500	5,600	3,500
4. Original paid-in capital	10,000	10,000		
10,000 × 120%			12,000	12,000
5. Holding gains on units sold:				
700 × ($15 − $10)		3,500		
700 × ($15 − 120% of $10)				2,100
6. Holding gains on units unsold:				
300 × ($15 − $10)		1,500		
300 × ($15 − 120% of $10)				900
7. Total assets:				
Cash (700 × $20)	$14,000	$14,000	$14,000	$14,000
Inventory (item 2 above)	3,000	4,500	3,600	4,500
Total Assets	$17,000	$18,500	$17,600	$18,500
8. Total equities				
Original paid-in capital (4)	$10,000	$10,000	$12,000	$12,000
Retained income (3)	7,000	3,500	5,600	3,500
Holding gains (5)	—	3,500	—	2,100
Holding gains (6)	—	1,500	—	900
Total equities	$17,000	$18,500	$17,600	$18,500

Sales − Variable Costs = CM

Cost-volume-profit = breakeven point = $\emptyset$ NI